See That You Are A True Inspiration

Written By

Quandriqurez R. Burkeen (Quan)

Unless otherwise indicated, all Scripture quotations are taken from
The New King James Version of the Bible. Copyright © 1979, 1980, 1982 by Thomas Nelson, Inc., Publishers. Used by permission.

The King James Version of the Bible in the public domain

Copyright © 2015 by Quandriqurez R. Burkeen

Cover designed by Exousia Graphics and Virtual Services

Printed in the United States of America

This book belongs to
_____

Do not read any further unless authorized by the person above to do so.

Dedication

Thank you, Jesus for the vision. This book is dedicated to my beautiful mother Debra Elaine Owens May 18, 1970 - August 11, 2012 and to my beloved father Barry Dean Burkeen March 26, 1964- February 13, 2013.

Introduction

I am a young man who is continually growing each and every day. I was born on January 04, 1994 to Debra Elaine Marks and Barry Dean Burkeen. I have been preaching and teaching the gospel since I was fourteen. As my grandmother tells me, God created me while I was in my mother's womb.

I have been gifted with a gift to help people by becoming an inspiration and empowerment to someone if not everybody. This has always been a great vision for me to write a book.

See That You Are A True Inspiration

Down through the years, I have been through storms, but my storms have yet to stop me. The toughest part of my life so far has been losing both of my parents at a young age. During high school, I watched my mother struggle with Amyotrophic Lateral Sclerosis (ALS), also known as Lou Gehrig's disease. After God called her home, I was relieved with joy in my heart. I also struggled with my father being sick due to a stroke that he had in 2002. Two years after my mother passed, my grandmother passed on my mother's birthday (May 18, 2015).

However, I choose to preach with great anointing as if nothing ever happened. No, I do not look like what I have been through, because I must continue to do the will of God. As I continue to do God's will, he will continue to bless my purpose and my future. Life teaches us things, but no matter what life brings we should always encourage ourselves.

You will never see me with my head low, because every day I know where my help comes from.

Losing both of my parents, my grandmother, and becoming divorced at such a young age changed my life dramatically. However, I still move forward, because I know that moving forward is necessary. One of the things losing my parents taught me was to value life and family, more each day.

Life comes with struggles that we must fight through. When the hardships come, understand that God will not put more on his children than we can bare. That is one of the greatest things about knowing God. Even in the dark days, he will take care of his people. During those storms we face, he still has the power to make the storms be at peace, because he will never leave us nor forsake us. You will never see me with my head hanging low.

This is not a story about my life, but this book is a book of encouragement and motivation. This book is to encourage others to continue to keep the faith. In this book, you will find many different things that helped me overcome many different impediments of life.

I love to challenge people into thinking a different way. While we have been through many things in life, we must learn to inspire and encourage ourselves. May God Bless you and continue to keep you.

Day One

Thought of the day: Strive to be better.

Strive: To try very hard to do or achieve something; to struggle in opposition

Many of us go through life not doing any better. Some people have become complacent doing nothing. Have you ever noticed the same people you went to high school with or graduated with in high school doing the same thing?

To get the things that you want in life you must work so that you are not complacent. You need to work toward something, because nothing can be given to you. In order to get somewhere and become better you must first strive.

Whether, you know it or not every day you are striving for something. To make it to the top, when you are working your hardest to achieve something, you have to struggle. I have many visions and I am yet still striving to get there. I know that my struggle will eventually take me there.

Striving is a challenge, but it helps you to do better in your life. Some of you want to better yourselves by becoming better parents, spouses, etc. That means you should allow God to prosper you to

See That You Are A True Inspiration

be better. Do not be ashamed to want to do better. You can do it if you want it. You will struggle once you are working your hardest for something.

If you want to do better than do better. Realize, in order to get better it will not come over night. It does not matter what people have to say. It is the struggle that will make you better. Setbacks have become comebacks and comebacks are not setbacks.

You must understand that it is okay to fall as long as you have the mindset of getting back up. Nevertheless, it is not okay to fail yourself. That is why they say failing is not an option. Even if you fall, God still forgives you. No matter where life takes you, God is always there. Do your best every single day.

Where there is no vision, the people perish: but he that keepeth the law, happy is he.

Proverbs 29: 18

Day One Reflections

Daily Prayer: If you are willing to do better for yourself Pray that God will open your heart and give you the mindset to strive for greatness.

What are you striving for?

_____
_____
_____
_____
_____

How would you make an effort of reaching your goals?

_____
_____
_____
_____
_____

What did God tell you when he gave you the vision?

_____
_____
_____

See That You Are A True Inspiration

<u>*Day Two*</u>

Thought of the day: I am made of greatness.

Greatness: full of; a notably large in size; relative largeness

Greatness starts with you. Greatness did not start with your relationships, family, or friends. Have you ever wondered how much greatness you are made of? God made no mistake creating you. In his creation, he gave you life and power to do beyond what you thought. Unfortunately, most people never realize that.

The purpose of greatness is to grow within you. Everyone has stumbled some-point in his or her lives. However, that just makes them even greater. If you prayed and believed that you are great then you can be great. The things that you prayed for, God will bless you with that and even more. Understand failures come with the intent of making you greater.

You may be struggling and cannot cope with the way things are going. You may not understand what God was doing when you had it all planned and he closed that door. Then you become choleric with God. Why get angry with God?

Understand that God will never put more on you than you can bare. There was a reason he closed the door. God knew that if you went through that door the outcome would not have been good. For that reason, he opened up an even greater door. God has a way of blessing you even greater. You may not deserve it, yet he still does it.

Greatness gives us all that opportunity to live above all things trying to take us down. Greatness gives you the ability to smile in the face of haters. Live above the lies that they told. Live on top of the world. Live above the fact that you were mistreated. Live above the past and live in the future.

You were made for greatness. You were made to do this. You were made for this purpose. In spite of what the world has done live above and walk into all

See That You Are A True Inspiration

of your greatness. Remember "with great power comes great responsibility".

But Jesus beheld them, and said unto them, "with men this is impossible; but with God all things are possible.

Matthew 19: 26

Day Two Reflections

Daily Prayer: Ask God to open your eyes so that you may see what you are truly made of?

What does greatness mean to you?

_____
_____
_____
_____
_____
_____

See That You Are A True Inspiration

Read John 4:4 and in your own words explain what this scripture means to you.

_____
_____
_____
_____
_____
_____

How would you plan to see your greatness?

_____
_____
_____
_____
_____
_____

Day Three

Thought of the day: Expand your faith

Faith: Strong belief or trust

Why is it that this one little word can mean so many things? Most of us have faith, but only a little. Sometimes, God will do things so that you really trust him. These things can make you question your faith

True Inspiration

sometimes. When you want things to happen you question God.

Dealing with faith, you must understand that God is able. Think of it this way. You sit in a chair having faith that it would hold you up, but you didn't think that it would break. The chair represents the fact that things can break things in your life unexpectedly. That is how faith works.

When things break, you should still be able to trust in God. I know for a fact that when you believe things start to happen. Sometimes you are in a situation where you are afraid. However, God encourages us to still trust in him.

People will never understand the way that they can expand. I can remember being in the hospital with my mother. The doctor gave her 24 hours to live. I had to expand my faith to understand that this too shall past. She had been suffering on this ventilator machine for two or three weeks. After that I received a phone call from whom I thought would be my (step) father. Little did I know, I was in for a surprise. It was my mother's voice and her first words were, "can you hear me"? Just by being able to hear her voice, I began to cry and smile. Because of my faith, God removed her from the intensive care unit. Later, she was released into the peace of her home. As I was dealing with her sickness, I wanted her to get well. I trusted in God for a miracle. I wanted to see her walk again. I wanted to enjoy more time with her. As I prayed for her one night, I said God let your will be done. I was simply saying God I trust you through what may happen. The next day he called her home.

Trust God in spite of bad and through the good. God will always be there despite the good or bad. Faith is something you cannot see, but you know it is there. So how can I rely on something that I cannot see? It is called relying on the word of God and the spirit. Just a little faith can do so much for us.

Understand that it is all in your faith. The bible says in James 2:26 that faith without work is dead. It is not good to pray or read the bible without any faith. Without faith you are ineffective and your gift is dead. If a person has no faith that person has then became a dead man walking.

Having Faith in God is what really makes us. People could not achieve if they did not have faith. Although you may want to be a doctor, lawyer, police, etc. there must be faith in doing these things. Faith is simply believing in God. Job is a perfect example of someone that has faith. Job lost everything he had, but continued to trust in God. Job trusted in God and God still made a way.

When there is no way out God still makes a way. When your back is up against the wall, God still makes a way. Bills are due and it seems as if you may not know what to do, as long as you trust in him and understand, nothing is too hard for God.

The thing most people do not know is that it was not my anointing nor was it my strength that helped me make it through the loss of both my parents at a young age. It was my faith that kept me. Sometimes we put our trust in the wrong people and the wrong things only to have the same results.

And Jesus said unto them, Because of your unbelief: verily I say unto you, if ye have faith a grain of a mustard seed, ye shall say unto this mountain, Remove hence to yonder place; and it shall remove; and nothing shall be impossible unto you.

Matthew 17:20

<u>*Day Three Reflections*</u>

Daily Prayer: Tell God how you trust in him and really mean it from your heart

Have you ever doubted God (if yes explain why and what were your doubts)?

_____
_____
_____
_____
_____

See That You Are A True Inspiration

What does faith mean to you?
_____
_____
_____
_____
_____
_____

Name some things you prayed over that never worked out?_____
_____
_____
_____
_____
_____

Day Four

Thought of the day: Your experience will make you better

Experience: The process of doing and seeing something and of having things happen to you: skill or knowledge that you get by doing something

See That You Are A True Inspiration

What is your experience? Most people have been asked this several times. Most of the time when you enter a new job the first question they will ask you "is are you experience?"

Experience is something we all have. Experience is the one thing that helps you to grow and to learn. Experience is the one thing that makes you better at what you do. Most of us can say we have had some bad experiences and mostly good experiences.

A horrible experience such as a divorce, a bad relationship, or even losing the ones closest to you is something that you can never prepare for. These type of experiences are life changing. This is the reason that God needed you to get the experience.

Do not blame others for something that you had no control over. It was never your fault. Take your experience with you everywhere you go. Many of us have the skill, but we need the experience. It is known as something that could be an eye opener.

See That You Are A True Inspiration

    Sometimes bad experiences happen due to you not listening or being disobedient. We must hit our head a few times to finally learn. If I could encourage you, allow me to say that the past was the past. I would not be the man I am now without my experiences. I never understood it, until God showed me that there was something wonderful in my experiences. You may not understand your experience, but it is always something wonderful out of. That is when you are finally able to challenge yourself to see the outcome. There is something better coming to make up for the bad experiences.

    Are you experienced enough to handle the triumphs? Some things have a way of teaching us a lesson. I can honestly say, I truly thank God for the many different experiences that I had to endure. Once you have experienced something, it will never go away.

    An experience is something that comes as a test of your strengths and weaknesses. If you are not prepared to handle experiences, then they will break you. Not to mention, it will pull you closer to God. Please understand that even in the midst of an experience, whether it is good or bad, God is always there to cover and shield us.

I have been asked the question several times, "how are you able to still do what you do after all the experiences you have overcome?" God knows it was not easy. The experiences that I have been through almost ripped me apart.

After the passing of my father, I really wanted to give up on everything. For some reason I could not seem to. God led a pastor that I know very well to call me to speak at his congregation. In your experiences of life, God has his hands on you.

To the ladies and gentlemen who have been through horrific experiences at a young age, please understand God created you for a beautiful purpose to do his work in the kingdom. Ladies and gentlemen, please let the things go that tried to destroy you or

True Inspiration

even keep you away from glorifying God. This is why I say your experience makes you better, even if you do not see this right now. You are better.

Now all these things happened unto them for examples: and they are written for our admonition, upon whom the ends of the world are come.

1 Corinthians 10: 11

Day Four Reflections

Daily Prayers: In times like these you need strength. Ask God to continue to give you strength to get through any difficult experiences.

What have you learned from your experiences?
_____
_____
_____
_____
_____

True Inspiration

What was the best experience?

_____
_____
_____
_____
_____

What was the worst experience for you?

_____
_____
_____
_____
_____

How has you experience changed you?

_____
_____
_____
_____
_____

Have you ever done anything that you would regret (explain)?

_____
_____
_____

Day Five

Thought of the day: Love has so much power

Love: A feeling of strong or strong constant affection

What is love? Love means a variety of things. It is something that can be very interesting. This four-letter word has a dynamic meaning. I do agree that it has been misused several times and in this society people are confused on the true meaning of love. Love is a powerful tool that can do a lot of good and so much damage.

Love can change a person spiritually, emotionally, physically, and mentally. People have been hurt or hurt others through love. On the other hand, some have hurt others, because they never really loved him or her. This happens once we get to close to the wrong people. Love does affect us and it effects the heart even worse. In order for you say that you love another person, you must accept in your heart that you really love him or her.

A person will play with someone's heart in order to get gratification for self. People use the term "I love you" in order to get sex, money, drugs or whatever have you. Before you can love others, you must first love yourself. Well, how do I love myself? There are many way to love yourself. Start by admiring you. Cherish everything you have done in life. Just because somebody said something does not mean it is true.

I cannot stress enough the importance of really loving yourself. Often times we place ourselves in situations where we love the wrong things and the people. Therefore, it falls back on us. Love is when a man such as Jesus will lay his life down for his people.

See That You Are A True Inspiration

Love can be very dangerous and addictive. If you really love something or someone, it shows. There is a difference between love and lust. Some people are in lust but not in love. Lust is known as a desire. Love will seek to desire the heart of man. It also seeks to understand. Before my divorce, I thought that I loved my ex-wife, only to understand that we may have been in lust because there wasn't any love there. The things that may seem great are not always great on the other side. The problem you have is that you love the wrong things for the wrong reason. I hear people say how they may not know exactly how to love.

However, everyone knows how to love. It just takes the right person to really bring that out of them. "Well I want to love him or her like they love me", some may say. Never try to love someone like they love you. You two are different; meaning your love for each other will be different. It will be as if he understands your heart or vice versa.

True Inspiration

Love cannot be established without a connection or bond. People will claim how they love you, but little do you know they really hate you. Love alongside hatred never adds up. The problem that I find is that too many people live with hatred in their heart. The bible tells us in Matthew 5:44 that we should love our enemies.

I want to encourage you to share love in your heart. In spite of what people have done to you. It does not matter what people have said or done, you must love them anyhow. It is easy to smile and say I love you. This is what will trick the adversary. Always remember to be careful, because love has so much power. True love gives you the key to a person's heart. Love a person, but make sure he/ she are the perfect one for you.

For God so loved the world that he gave his only begotten Son, that whosoever believeth in him should not perish, but have everlasting life.

John 3:16

Day Five Reflections

Daily Prayer: Allow God to search your heart and replace anything that is ungodly with love

What does love mean in your own words?

_____
_____
_____
_____
_____

Have you been in a place where you could not love yourself?

_____
_____
_____
_____
_____

When in a relationship have you thought you loved someone but he/she was not the one?

_____
_____
_____

True Inspiration   *See That You Are A*

_____
_____
_____

What did you learn through love?

_____
_____
_____
_____
_____

<u>*Day Six*</u>

Thought of the day: Hush it up

Hush: when nothing is said or is coming out the mouth verbally

Many of us like myself love to speak. Speaking too much can cause you to miss your blessing. God cannot bless in mess. You may have been on the cusp of receiving a great blessing, until you began speaking the wrong things, or speaking against people.

It is a shame that people will talk about others while their back is turned. Again, God cannot bless you while you are in the process of speaking negativity in someone's life. Know that you can bless or curse someone through your words. The tongue is the deadliest weapon of all.

Any physical object can kill someone. However, with the tongue a man can kill someone in multiple ways. The tongue can kill mentally, spiritually, emotionally, and even physically. A thing so little and so deadly, people fail to realize that there is much power in a tongue.

In other words if one wants something to happen, it shall be in your favor once it has been spoken. Even the church is guilty of this. I say that, because people will sit in the church discouraging others while the Pastor is trying to encourage them. People love to sit in church just to gossip. Why would anyone want to crush the heart of others and deter their dreams? People speak negative against others because they have not took the time to think about their words.

Instead of trying to speak negative, speak positive into your life and others. I never understood how people are able to live with themselves starting rumors, lying on others, or even starting mess. This is all things you encounter. It never feels good when you are the one getting lied on, or talked about.

People are so quick to say the wrong things about someone else, but want to get aggressive when it is done to them. Please check yourself. All of these things were done to Jesus. They lied on him, talked about him, cursed him, and even put the name of Jesus down.

How can one do so much damage with this? My grandmother and my beloved mother always told me that "if you are not going to say anything good, then do not say anything at all". The sad thing about that is that no one will ever understand that. Those words can be said a million times and people still will not catch it.

See That You Are A True Inspiration

I am not saying not to defend yourself. However, there are ways of doing that by simply blessing one with I love you and God bless you. The moral of the story is that sometimes it is best to be quiet. Be quick to think, but slow to speak. It is all about how something is said.

Just remember once something has been said it cannot be taken back. This means chose your words wisely. Watch your tone. Watch how you respond to others because it can come back on you.

A man's belly shall be satisfied with the fruit of his mouth; and with the increase of his lips shall be filled. Death and life are in the power of the tongue: and they that love it shall eat the fruit thereof.

Proverbs 18:20-21

Day Six Reflections

Daily Prayer: Today you need to ask God to forgive for anything that you have said ungodly. Also, ask

See That You Are A True Inspiration

God to help you be quick to think but yet slow to speak.

What was the worst thing ever said to you?

_____
_____
_____
_____
_____
_____

What is / was the worst thing you have ever said?

_____
_____
_____
_____
_____
_____

How will you encourage others along with yourself?

_____
_____
_____
_____
_____
_____

True Inspiration

How will you plan to bite your tongue or be quiet?

_____
_____
_____
_____
_____

Day Seven

Thought of the day: Learn to be wise

Wise / wisdom: having or showing some wisdom or knowledge usually from learning or experiencing many things: based on good reasoning or information: showing good sense or judgment: marked by deep understanding and keen discernment.

Being wise is a very important attribute of life. Most people will never understand the difference between knowledge and wisdom. Although the two may sound similar, they are very different. Knowledge is based on an accumulation of facts that one has learned. Knowledge is acquired through study, research, or investigation.

See That You Are A True Inspiration

Wisdom is the ability to discern and judge, which aspects of that knowledge are true, right, lasting, and applicable to your life. It is the ability to apply that knowledge to a greater scheme of life. Wisdom is deeper than knowledge. It is knowing the meaning or reason about why something is, and what it could mean to a person's life.

Having wisdom is like being able to break down a complicated math problem in order to get the full understanding. Knowledge speaks while wisdom listens and observes.

As I was a young child, I can remember listening to my grandfather talk to me dealing with several things. We would always laugh about many things. My grandfather would express such wisdom to me. He was instilling the gift of wisdom in me at a young age. Due to him experiencing many things, he was passing what he knew down to me. Now that I am older, I can say that I am wiser.

See That You Are A True Inspiration

Every day you are in a process of growing and learning. As an adult I have made wrong decisions that later on in life came back on me. The things you do today could affect you for the rest of your life. A wise man will really think about his decision before he makes it.

So that means you should be wise in your decision making process of life. In order to be wise, a person must learn from all the flaws he or she has made. I highly respect those with big degrees. The question that I ask is, have you applied yourself? Have you applied what was learned in the classroom to life? Again, I say wisdom is when you are able to apply the things that you have learned in life.

Life has made you understand some things. The possession of materialistic things will never make a person wise. It is always good to prioritize. It is unfortunate that you can gain a lifetime of knowledge, yet never see wisdom in it. Wisdom is

True Inspiration

the key to everything in life. Having common sense is just as important as having wisdom.

But the wisdom that is from above is first pure, then peaceable, gentle, and easy to be in-treated, full of mercy and good fruits, without partiality, and without hypocrisy.

James 3: 17

Day Seven Reflections

Daily Prayer: Ask God in helping you to gain wisdom in areas where you lack

What does it mean to have wisdom?

_____
_____
_____
_____
_____

Where does wisdom come from?

True Inspiration   *See That You Are A*

_____
_____
_____
_____
_____
_____

How can a person gain wisdom?

_____
_____
_____
_____
_____

Day Eight

Thought of the day: Open your eyes

Eyes: an ability to understand and appreciate something seen: point of view

Eyes are something that every creature has. Eyes are a gift given to you to see. Having said that what exactly does it mean to open your eyes? When a baby is born, it is born into the darkness of this world.

Being a newborn baby, it will see nothing, but darkness until it finally opens it eyes to see the light.

When you really open your eyes, God will reveal several things to you that were impossible to see. People will do everything to avoid the signs that something isn't right. Some people have seen darkness for quite some time. You want to see the light, but all you see is the darkness of this world.

Some people may be very well living in darkness right now. They want to cover it up and eventually see the light, but it is still dark. I want to encourage you to make today your last day of being in darkness. Make today your last day covered in darkness.

Now it is time to open your eyes to see the light. Open your eyes so that you are finally able to see what God has in store for you. A good percentage of people will refuse to open their eyes, because they may just be accustomed to the way things are or even afraid to see the things that God has in store. A lot of

True Inspiration

times we will see things that was not intended to see. It confuses me when I hear stories of people asking God for a great spouse, a new house, a new job, or a new car. The reason that it confuses me is because when God gives you these things you then turn them down.

With that being said, you will go through the entire process again of asking God for these things. Open your eyes to see the bigger picture. People will try to force many things such as happiness, yet cannot seem to find it due to them not wanting it bad enough.

Your eyes cannot see the things that you do not want. Stop being blind to what God is trying to reveal unto you. Open your eyes to see yourself, your heart, and to understand who you are.

People are so quick to see ugly in someone, but cannot see ugly in themselves. With opened eyes, the ability to see things come natural. Opened eyes give a person the ability to see someone's heart.

See That You Are A True Inspiration

Some people are in a particular place where they have not yet opened their eyes. Before moving somewhere, you will need a revelation from God. Take time to ask God where he needs you to be.

Often time's people jump into relationships not knowing what is on the other side. Often times people jump into relationships to allow sex and their feelings to get in the way. A person will find true happiness once they have really opened their eyes to see all God's many blessing. With your eyes you should admire the beauty in what you see.

The Lord openeth the eyes of the blind: the Lord raiseth them that are bowed down: the Lord loveth the righteous.

Psalms 146: 08

Day Eight Reflections

See That You Are A True Inspiration

Daily Prayer: There are many things that God wants you to see. He has something good waiting for you. However, you must be willing to open your eyes clearly. Ask God to allow to see that something wonderful that you have never seen before.

What are some things that you may want to see?

_____
_____
_____
_____
_____

What are some things that you fail to see?

_____
_____
_____
_____
_____

How will you begin to open your eyes?

_____
_____
_____
_____
_____

See That You Are A True Inspiration

What things do you see in yourself?
_____
_____
_____
_____
_____
_____
—

What do you fail to see in yourself?
_____
_____
_____
_____
_____
_____

Day Nine

Thought of the day: I must have a strong finish

Finish: To bring something to an end

See That You Are A True Inspiration

What does it mean to have a strong finish? Having a strong finish means that you are very determined to be great. In order to finish, you must come out on top of whatever became detrimental to you. This means working toward some things in life. When you graduate high school the next step is either college, military, or a career.

Most people move into their area of focus after graduating college. It will certainly be hard at first, because you must find a way to get your foot in the door. Planning should be done in order to get to that place of success. If you fail to plan then you will plan to fail. It is as simple as that. Ask yourself these questions: How will I move into my focus? Who will stop me? Do I have a backup plan? These questions will help you determine your finish. I am a firm believer that God will never put more on you than you can bare, but there must be some impediments to climb over before going anywhere. The race is useless if we aren't running for something.

Understand that even when you are in tight situation he is still there. God still does not leave you. Most of you are guilty of telling yourself that you cannot do something. That means that you will not because your mindset will not allow you to do it.

Everything starts with you and your mindset. This means that if a person has the wrong the mindset, they will have the wrong outcome. For example as Peter began walking on water he had everything going well for him until he lost focus on God. Wherever God may take you in life, you cannot lose focus.

Haters will say and do whatever they may please, but you cannot worry about your haters. The ones closest to us should be our main priority. They are the main ones wanting to see you fail. It gives them the opportunity to continue to put you down. A hater could be anyone closest to you such as a best friend or a family member. Sad to say but it is very true.

See That You Are A True Inspiration

While others are putting you down, continue to walk into your purpose. Continue to walk in God's divine favor. If the vision is there then go for it. God sees you waiting at the door. Now how do I get in? You have the key, because you are the key to success. I understand that success is a must.

Wait on God, once God opens that door run through it. Continue to knock on the door of success until it is finally open. If God be for us, then who can stand against us, nor shall any man stand in your way. People need to understand their key focus. Focus on yourself before anything else.

STOP ALLOWING OTHERS TO TELL YOU WHAT CAN AND CANNOT BE DONE IN YOUR LIFE. STOP ALLOWING PEOPLE TO DICTATE YOUR LIFE. AS A MATTER OF FACT, STOP ALLOWING PEOPLE TO STAND OVER YOU.

I loved when my mother would always say "I must endure until the end". It is hard for you right now and you do not understand what is happening, but endurance helps us to finish the race. It's very important that you learn to endure the challenge by stepping out on faith. I will take it until I make it. God is able to do exceedingly, abundantly, and above all you may ask or think. It shall come to pass. The things that you have been praying for and waiting on shall come to pass. Abundance is near.

I returned, and saw under the sun, that the race is not to the swift, nor the battle to the strong, neither yet bread to the wise, nor yet riches to men of understanding, nor yet favour to men of skill; but the time and chance happeneth to them all.

Ecclesiastes 9:11

Day Nine Reflections

Daily Prayer: Ask God to allow you to finish your dreams with the purpose to become successful

What is something you may be waiting on?

See That You Are A True Inspiration

_____
_____
_____
_____

What are your long-term goals?

_____
_____
_____
_____

Is there anything in your way that you may feel is stopping you?

_____
_____
_____
_____

Day Ten

Thought of the day: Forgive them anyhow

Forgive: the act of excusing or pardoning others in spite of their slights, shortcomings, and errors.

See That You Are A True Inspiration

Many times, you are in situations where you have to forgive someone for something they have done to you. The problem is that sometimes people do not want to forgive others, because they are still holding a grudge on something. It is better to forgive than to live in pain suffering.

I never understood ones who can be willing to forgive, yet still hold a grudge within their heart. Instead of forgiving, people will ask that their adversary be cursed. It would not be forgiving if you are still holding a grudge. It is imperative that you learn to forgive.

Some people still have the same hatred within their heart from several years ago. It may take you awhile to heal from something, but you still should forgive. As I was dealing with the pain of my divorce, forgiveness was not easy. However, I finally came into realization that I must forgive.

See you must understand that is was God that forgave you even you turned your back on him

See That You Are A True Inspiration

several times. Dealing with pain is never easy. Dealing with people lying on you is never easy. Someone may have done nothing wrong. Therefore, forgiveness is a must. Man will do everything that they can. It is even worse for the children of God. It is always the ones that we least expect.

Your own family will be the quickest to stab you in the back. Even the church will smile in your face and cut you. For example, even Jesus being our Lord and savior managed to forgive. Jesus was a man that done nothing wrong, but men of this world did everything to him.

People have done all this to me, but I still forgive. Not only do I encourage people to forgive, but I also encourage people to pray for those who despise you. While praying for your adversaries, God will allow them to be at your feet (Luke 20:43) . God will also turn everything around for your good. If it happened to Jesus then whom are you that it will not happen to you.

Forgiveness is letting go. Many people live with what happened in the past. They find themselves suffering, because they have not let go of the past. The past makes you who you are today. The past makes you a better person.

Do not blame mother, father, uncle, brother, aunt, or sister. Do not even blame yourself for whatever happened in your past. Understand that there comes a time where God will heal the broken heart. Move on from that place of depression. Move on from that place of hurt.

People will forgive, but it will certainly be hard to forget. I have been in many places where I had to forgive. Forgiveness does not make you less of a person. It comes deeply from within the heart. Forgiveness will help make you a better person. After Jesus was placed on the cross, having to withstand everything that man had done to him He said, "Father forgive them for they know not what they have done". They do not understand that I am a child of the king, but father forgive them. They don't understand the things that they have put me through, but father forgive them. They will never understand that you are a child of the King. They do not understand it right now, because their mind is not focused on your feelings. They are conformed to the world. They are not for you knowing that you belong to God.

The circumstances that people put you in will get better for you. I know what it feels like being lied on, talked about, cursed, bruised, etc. I also know what it feels like having doors shut in your face literally. I have dealt with family talking about me when my back was turned. I have also dealt with church members attempting to put me down. However, I am still able to forgive.

Maybe it is just the type that I am. Here is the thing you need to learn, a person shall never live with un-forgiveness in the heart. People always make the same mistakes and later ask God to forgive them.

See That You Are A True Inspiration

Even though you may fail God several times, he still forgives you. The choice of forgiveness is left up to you.

The said Jesus "Father, forgive them; for they know not what they do. And they parted his raiment, and cast lots.

Luke 23:34

Day Ten Reflections

Daily Prayer: Ask God to give you the strength to forgive those you have despise you. Also, ask God to give you the strength to let go of whatever you may been holding onto from the past.

In your own words explain the word "forgiveness".

_____
_____
_____
_____

See That You Are A True Inspiration

Why is so important to forgive?

Are you still holding on to something that happened in the past?

Have you forgave everyone in your life that caused you grief?

Day Eleven

Thought of the day: Being in the flesh vs being in feelings

Flesh: human nature: having passions

Feelings: an emotional state or reaction: the undifferentiated background of one's awareness considered apart from any identifiable sensation, perception, or thought

How can a person be in the flesh while being emotional? Flesh and feelings are those natural things that we all have. They both can be controlled. Some people believe that it is hard to control their feelings. Have you ever had someone ask you to do something and you began to buck up at that person? Well, that is what the flesh is doing when God wants you to do something. You will buck, because you know that it is true and you could care less of hearing it.

Flesh is considered a spiritual warfare. Sins are committed when someone is in their flesh. Most people are in the flesh when they are lonely, depressed, or even hurting. The desire, opportunity, and love for something could all be involved with things of the world. These things will cause you to depart from God. People attempt to make excuses that their flesh is weak. The flesh is something that everyone wrestles with daily.

It can be hard to do good when evil is waiting, but you must learn to turn from evil. Better yet, you must learn to turn away from your wicked ways. Even the most anointed have made mistakes. The flesh is controlled by praying, fasting, and studying the word of God. While at the emotional stage our flesh is seeking something or something in someone else.

When a person is in the flesh, he or she can be "in love" with things. This can cause him or her to depart from God. When you are emotional, you are vulnerable. The enemy will bring temptations, but it is up to you to decide whether you want the temptations or not.

See That You Are A True Inspiration

I believe people should allow God to bring the flesh under subjection. Therefore, it can be moved out the way because God is still sustaining you. Which means that He isn't finished with you. People are quick to blame the adversary for everything they do. That is when you cry " oh God it is me ". Again, I say while being in your feelings you must pray daily in order to keep your flesh and your feelings from being able to overtake you. Being in flesh could be fighting an addiction that is hard to get rid of. Every time the addiction is thought of, the flesh WILL eat man alive to satisfy the desire. If you desire your flesh, then your flesh desires you every time.

People will pray and ask God to forgive them only to turn around to do the same thing. That is backwards. Whatever you were doing, it is time to come out of that. Do not even think about allowing the flesh to stop what God has done for you or the things that he is doing. Sometimes at your most vulnerable points, you need God to sit on you to

See That You Are A True Inspiration

prevent you from committing anything against his will.

For I know that in me (that is, in my flesh,) dwelled no good thing: for to will is present with me; but how to perform that which is good I find not.

Romans 7:8

Day Eleven Reflections

Daily Prayer: Ask God to give you strength and power over the flesh. Even when the flesh may become weak you are still able to control it.

What are some things you may be wrestling with?
_____
_____
_____
_____
_____

How do you plan to let go of these things?
_____
_____
_____

True Inspiration   *See That You Are A*

_____
_____

How can a person control the flesh?
_____
_____
_____
_____
_____

What ways can you control your feelings?
_____
_____
_____
_____
_____

<u>Day Twelve</u>

Thought of the day: Wait on it to happen

Wait: to stay in a place until an expected event happens or in hope that something will happen soon

See That You Are A True Inspiration

Have you ever heard the saying "it's a waiting game?" Another example would be standing in line. They say do not push. Sometimes we are waiting and try to rush into our blessings. Most of us including myself do not like to wait. We have the bad habit of waiting for something. It becomes to where we want to rush into something unexpected not knowing the outcome. In this day and time, people will even attempt to rush God.

God has the ability to slow down time or speed it up. This is something that Pastor Ernest Lemon said. I tried to figure out the meaning of that several times. Think of it like this, it may not be time yet for whatever you want to happen. God has a way of slowing you down when you are moving too fast. Everything works on God's timing. He could either be speeding the process up or slowing it down.

God slows you down so you are not in situations that you will regret. Sometimes you will find yourself praying on the things you want several times, it is the process that you must endure. We all have big dreams, big hopes, and big futures. Some people will never understand the reason behind waiting.

You are waiting with a purpose, as well as for a purpose. God has you waiting, because greatness is coming in due time. You may be waiting, because you may need to experience a little more. You may be waiting due to you lack of ability to understand your purpose. You may even be waiting for the right things to happen at the wrong time, while others are waiting due to lack of growth being a factor.

Both of my sisters have stressed this four letter word to me several times. It is important to wait and sometimes slow down. People will always ask God for a new house, a new car, a new job, or even a significant other. There is nothing wrong with asking God for these things.

Just know that whatever you are waiting for is soon to come. The more waiting you do comes with a better purpose. You may be at the wrong place at the wrong time due to failure of waiting, which is something to think about. So while in the waiting process some things and possibly people may have to be removed. You can cause yourself more grief by failing to wait. God has to remove the old factors (things and people) in order to bless us with new beginnings. Those things and people can be detrimental. Relationships and jobs that you were involved had no meaning at all. These are examples of rushing into something that God was fixing. So, if you are in a place of waiting allow God to finish what he wants to do in your life and heart. There is no need to stay somewhere that has no meaning or a purpose for you.

If you are waiting, then wait until God moves you into that place where he needs you to be. Continue to stay humble in your waiting phase. I certainly believe that there is a time for everything. It is important to allow yourself not to move from the place where God has you placed. You are there for a reason. You want many things to occur in your life. However, the one thing that you may fail to understand is that God has you in your waiting process. The thing you must understand is that you cannot rush God.

But they that wait upon the Lord shall renew their strength; they shall renew their strength; they shall mount up with wings as eagles; they shall run, and not be weary; and they shall walk, and not faint. Isaiah 40:31

<u>Day Twelve Reflections</u>

Daily Prayer: Remember to keep your eyes focused on God by asking him to all you to really be patient. This way he is able to really bless you.

What are some things that you are waiting on?

_____
_____
_____
_____
_____

True Inspiration

Why do you believe that it is so hard for people to wait?

_____
_____
_____
_____
_____

While waiting what are things you could work on?

_____
_____
_____
_____
_____

Day Thirteen

Thought of the day: Never judge a book by its cover

Judge: To form an opinion about something or someone after careful thought which can be good or bad

See That You Are A True Inspiration

Have you ever had to sit in front of a judge and explain to him or her what was done and why? Going in front of a judge is never a pleasant feeling. A judge can be intimidating. People fear them, because their fate is in the power of the judge's hands.

When people judge others, they have formed an opinion about something or someone. Many of us live with opinions, but not the truth. It is never good to form an opinion about something or someone that does not concern you. That means quit judging others with no facts.

People have the tendency to judge others before they meet them. Judging others is an everyday struggle that we all face. People get judged based on their appearance and performance in certain things. This could also be known as bullying someone. Some people had suicidal thoughts because of someone really degrading their character. Most people will judge others and start rumors or something that is based off hearsay. I am sure many of you have books that you have never read laying around collecting dust. Understand that you will not know the true meaning of that book, until you have opened it to see what is on the inside.

The judge will never see or understand what you have been through. The judge will never understand the pain in your heart. The judge sees what is on the outside. He or she will never understand that you are trying to do right. They may give you an outside label, because of some things in your life that they are trying to so call "fix".

When people judge you, it brings your self-esteem down. The ones, as the judge, feel confident in their decision. God spoke to me saying, "You're nothing on the outside, but I am getting ready to fix the inside". Encourage people, because you are literally writing your own book entitled "**The Book of Life**". Stop to think about this. There is one judge you will never be able to hide from.

He is same judge that you will never be able to run from. This judge never needs a warrant to make his final decision. The same judge sees everything you do in life. That means if people continue to judge others based on the outer appearance they too will be judged accordingly.

God will care less about the final clothes you are wearing in the casket. God sees your heart. If your heart is not right, then I would encourage you to get your heart together. We all have a judge, but too many of us spend time sticking our nose where it does not belong. This is the reason people feel the need to judge others.

Judge not, that ye be not judged. For with what judgment ye judge, shall be judged: and with measure ye mete, it shall be measured to you again.

Matthew 7: 1 & 2

See That You Are A True Inspiration

<u>Day Thirteen Reflections</u>

Daily Prayer: Ask God to remove anything that may be considered judging

What is judging?

Have you ever judged someone in the wrong way?

Have you ever been judged in the wrong way?

See That You Are A True Inspiration

_____
_____
_____

How can a person live without judging other?

_____
_____
_____
_____
_____

Day Fourteen

Thought of the day: There is always a better way

Have you ever wondered how something can be done? If there was only a better way that I could do this? Thomas Edison an American inventor and businessman gave us the motivation that there is a better way do something which means we need to find it. This is something we can apply to our daily lives. Create a better way by doing something new.

See That You Are A True Inspiration

Many of us are doing something which may be good, but we refuse to take that better option. Again, a lot of people are afraid of doing something new. They are afraid to face their fears or the challenge of something. We could be on our jobs, or at home and fail to realize there is always a better way. Some things we do can bring about change. People are so quick to give up on something very important, due to the better way that hasn't been found.

A better way equals a better life. Quit spending time going into things the wrong way. Couples, quit spending time loving each other the wrong way. Go and find your better way. The way that will perfectly fit your needs.

Here is an amazing tip for your information! The thing(s) that you do today can affect you for the remainder of your life. Decisions can change our life; whether they are excellent or even poor. Find that better way in your life and apply to whatever you need to.

See That You Are A True Inspiration

But covet earnestly the best gifts: and yet shew I unto you a more excellent way.

1 Corinthians 12: 31

Day Fourteen Reflections

Daily Prayer: There is always a better way. There is always something better. Ask God on today to allow to take the better way.

How can you improve things in your life?

_____
_____
_____
_____
_____
_____

What are some things you believe are better for you?

_____
_____
_____
_____

Explain your different way to be creative in doing things?

See That You Are A True Inspiration

_____
_____
_____
_____
_____

Day Fifteen

Thought of the day: Where is your humility?

Humility: defined as a freedom from arrogance that grows out of the recognition that all we have and all we are comes from God.

Where is your humbleness? This was my very first sermon I preached at New Harvest Family Church in Columbia TN. There are many qualities one must have in order to be completely humble. Some people are at that stage where they are there but not completely there. Humility is in ordinance with being obedient .Learning to be wiser due to growth gives you the opportunity to change your outlook on different things. Our maturity plays a significant role in our humbleness.

See That You Are A True Inspiration

The more you grow, learn, and experience the more you become humble. Humbleness comes when you are completely able to understand why things happen. It comes when you completely bring your flesh under subjection. Being humble is a key tool as we live our life. This means moving yourself and things out the way such as flesh, pride, or the egoistic way as well as being more submissive to God and less assertive. Meaning, everything cannot go your way. That also means that you should be more submissive to God.

Independence is a form of pride. It will get you every time if you are not careful. Your attitude toward people is all in ordinance with being humble. People will allow pride to get in the way of what God is saying. A humble person will watch their reactions. They will have the tongue to speak wise.

Life has a very interesting way of making you humble if you cannot be humble. Things will happen in order for you to humble yourself. Humbleness is something you do not get within one day. Somethings you go through can bring this into your lives. Believe me, when I say this, when God says it is time to move then you should move. God will block blessings from a disobedient person.

The thing I see the most is people disobeying God. That is due to the flesh speaking and making the decisions. Even Jesus had to humble himself. For this reason, we all should obey the spirit. I am sure God has been knocking on someone's heart for quite some time. The reason that God does these things is to test your humility and see if you will respond. God could have the things you have prayed for just by the response to him.

As a humble person you must began to carry yourself in a certain manner, and not do or say certain things. Speaking of making wise judgments, I must say this, most people want be humble. I applaud everyone that has grown into humility. However, some people think only of themselves or they are arrogant. It is almost as if they have the mentality that they are better. See no one is better than anyone else. Another trait of humbleness is having the spirit of forgiveness.

So remember what makes a humble person are things based on attitude, growth, learning, understanding, moving pride, moving flesh, forgiveness, and obedience. Another thing that will make someone humble is the way that he or she speaks to others. If you cannot be humble, God will humble you. That is something that you do not want him to do.

And being found in fashion as a man, he humbled himself, and became obedient unto death, even the death of the cross. Philippians 2:8

Day Fifteen Reflections

Daily Prayer: If God is calling you or telling you to move elsewhere then do it by asking God to allow humbleness to show and disobedience to cease from this point.

What does the word "humble" mean to you (explain in your own words)?

_____
_____
_____
_____
_____

Have you ever heard God calling you?

_____
_____
_____
_____
_____

How did you respond (negative or positive)?

_____
_____
_____

See That You Are A True Inspiration

_____
_____
_____

Would you call yourself humble (explain)?
_____
_____
_____
_____
_____

What traits do you have that would make you completely humble?
_____
_____
_____
_____
_____

Day Sixteen

Thought of the day: Watch who you surround yourself with

Surround: a transitive verb meaning, to be on every side of (something or someone): moving close to: or to be closely related or connected to something.

See That You Are A True Inspiration

Will you be surrounded? The word surround shows action. Surround can be good or bad. On the good side, it could be everything you wanted. On the bad side, it can be annoying. Most people will surround themselves around people or things that never had a value within their heart or life. Our spirits will begin to connect to those that surround us. They will start thinking alike or maybe doing the same things. The not so good people that are close to us can pressure someone into doing something that should not be condoned.

First, allow me to say you must be careful who you surround yourself with. People today want to associate with your life so they can know what is going on. Even the closest ones to you that you think you can trust are the first to turn on you. People told me how they could have been dead or in jail, because of hanging with the wrong crowd or being in wrong the place at the wrong time.

Now, there are people in this world who want to see you strive for endeavors in many ways. The same people will motivate you daily. These people are the ones you need in your life. The people that you surround yourself with can be good or detrimental, having said that, it is best to pick your circle wisely. Some people want to see you fall and fail, so they can laugh at you and encourage you to fall even more.

People will always impact your life, because you give them room to do so. Allow me to say, if no one is in your life that will motivate or help you become better then motivate yourself. For example, women love being surrounded by love, but some men do not know how to surround a woman with his full love. Another example is Jesus who surrounds us every single day. He cares for us. Jesus protects you by showing grace and mercy. He is one whom we follow.

See That You Are A True Inspiration

These great people surround you every day. They can also enlighten many things within your life. The old saying, "we either met for a reason or either you are a blessing or a lesson" means so much today. Negativity is not something you need in your life. People should fill your mind with positive thoughts every day if you allow them.

I must say the people you are around can influence you spiritually. If they pull you away from Christ, then they are no good for you. Always watch your surroundings. We as people should be careful and watchful as to the ones we allow in our lives. Some people you hang with are a true definition of a snake. They are the same ones ready for you to mess up. They are the ones quick to bite you and poison your lives.

They are everywhere. The snakes are on your job, at home, and somewhere in your best friends. You cannot allow people to continue to manipulate you. Believe it or not manipulation is the one thing you are way too good for.

Beware of dogs, beware of evil workers, and beware of the concision.

Philippians 3: 2

Day Sixteen Reflections

Daily Prayer: Ask God on this day to place people in your life for a purpose.

How can someone affect you?
_____
_____
_____
_____
_____

Are you currently facing difficult things with your circle of friends?
_____
_____
_____

True Inspiration   *See That You Are A*

_____

_____

What qualities do you have to make you a great person or a great friend?

_____
_____
_____
_____
_____

Day Seventeen

Thought of the day: It is time to walk out of it.

Walk: the act of progressing toward somewhere else: to pursue a course of action or way of life: standing with appearance: taking steps out of something.

What does it mean to walk out something? This is very interesting. Everything you do is done by taking a risk. As you live your daily life, you walk into many things you never knew that you were walking into. You became a part of something, not knowing good from bad.

Sometimes you walk into your own problems. You walk into things unexpectedly, which will cause heartaches, headaches, and stress. It could be as simple as living in debt. Most people do not know simply being faithful to God solves financial situations.

Some people have the mentality to question God. You should never have the mindset to question his works. These things will overtake you in your wellbeing, if you allow them. People should never want to live a stressful life, but an eventful or felicitous life. Your life should suit you for a purpose.

You must began to walk out of some things. In spite of dealing with life, you should be persistent in what you do. It amazes me that people will stay somewhere that they are not needed and these same people will stay there knowing they are not welcomed. Stress, heartaches, and headaches will then creep its way into our life and unhappiness begins.

Walking out of something that meant no good may be best for a person. For example, many people stay in relationships for the fun of it. They are there to play; there are no feelings, no emotions, and no love. You must understand when it comes to a relationship and it is time to go, then it is time to go. Why are you there? What are you getting from it? These are questions that can be applied to any relationship. It's a shame that people will stay somewhere in lust.

I spent many days trying to understand the reason my ex-wife did not want to be married. Some people do not want you or want to be with you. Which is something you cannot understand. They may feel you are in their way. It could also be your character, or jealousy. Go to something better and worth it. Go to a place where you and your time are valued. Bishop T.D Jakes, pastor of The Potters

See That You Are A True Inspiration

House in Dallas Texas said, "Waste my anything, but do not waste my time".

Many people will say it is never good to walk away from your problems. It may not be good to walk away from your problems, but it is better to give it all to God for he understands and cares for us. Use this as tool to walk out of your problems. Sometimes it best to take a break and breathe.

We all have things we are facing. However, understand that when you walk out something it does you good. That means you can never look back. Some people will never understand the accomplishments they can make until they walk out of an abusive relationship, addiction, debt, baby daddy or baby mama drama etc.

It is no wonder that success has not come. You want to deal with something. You want to be a part of something that has no significant meaning. For the most part, most of you stay due to something

See That You Are A True Inspiration

telling you it is not quite time to let go with the mindset that you are getting something good out of it.

For example, people will be quick to walk into the club, but will not walk into church once. People will walk into bad habits, but make excuses not to find a good habit. Some are in conundrum or sticky situation, because of something they did, something they became accustomed to, not letting go, or wanting to be difficult. Now they are stuck in mess.

Allow me to elaborate. When I say walk out of something, I am not referring to a job or education. It is not in your best interest to walk out on the two, unless God has given you something else and told you to move. Many people will stay expecting something only to get nothing. Never be in a place always expecting, especially if you are in relationship or on the job. Most things will happen naturally.

I find that many people look for something in things such as honors or awards. Please understand this God has a special divine purpose for us all. Why should you be unhappy for the remainder of your life? Then you slow yourself down saying," I did not ask to be unhappy, I thought this was happiness when it never was".

Some people think that they are too good for you. You do not understand them and they can never seem to understand you. Walk into the things that God has for you and walk out of everything that the adversary thought he cost you. Stop trying to stay there and fix it

If we live in the spirit, let us also walk in the spirit.

Galatians 5: 25

Day Seventeen Reflections

Daily Prayer: Some things we just have to walk out of. Whatever is hindering you from doing the work of the Lord ask him to allow you to walk out and walk into your divine purpose for your life to be able to walk into something supernatural.

See That You Are A True Inspiration

What are some things in your life that are hindering you?

_____
_____
_____
_____
_____

How can you walk out of something doing you no good?

_____
_____
_____
_____
_____

Explain the success factors you feel are behind your walking out process?

_____
_____
_____
_____
_____

In your own words what does "walking out" mean to you?

_____

See That You Are A True Inspiration

_____
_____
_____
_____
_____

How would you encourage someone to walk out?

_____
_____
_____

<u>Day Eighteen</u>

Thought of the day: Let your light shine

Shine: standing out: glowing: give off light

Did you know we live in a world full of evil and hatred? The reason for this is that most people are full of darkness. People may look appeasing or well-dressed on the outside, but they have so much evil within their heart. A smile can even be deceiving.

Well how can a smile be deceiving? A person will smile in your face, so you are unable to see them for who they really are. I would encourage everyone not to be the victim of this. Being covered in darkness makes people look ugly. It does not matter how much make up one may put on, or how attractive he or she may be. Darkness never looks good on anyone, because it will give them an ugly personality.

Darkness is when a person lives with hate in their heart. Darkness can be classified as having a horrible attitude toward one person. Why would someone want wrap himself or herself into this? As if, people do not have enough problems every day. The same people are always wondering why nothing isn't ever going well. We live in a dark world. People are killing others for no apparent reason at all. People are sleeping around with married people. More violence is erupting in the world. I wonder when will the light shine. When will the church and the community come together? When will the killing stop?

In times like these we ask the question where is God? Little do you know, he is shining in this midst of everything going on. However, more people have turned on Christ. People have quit following him. You must allow your light to shine in midst of what people are doing to you. You must allow your light to shine despite being lied on, talked about, or backstabbed. Despite any horrific event that happened in the past, you must allow your light to shine.

One day everyone will come to reality. They do not understand due to them being dirty. It is what is on the inside that counts. I am reminded how God began to create the world. Everything was dark. God said, "Let there be light". In other words, there needs some sort of light here. For example, when you arrive to your house you must turn the light on to see. One who can easily allow the light to shine is one who shows it. When a person's light really shines, the person will glow. Create a loving environment when someone talks about you, lies on you, or puts your name in the dirt. Today is the day to allow your light

See That You Are A True Inspiration

to really shine. Once a person starts to evaluate him or herself the light can start to shine more each day.

Neither do men light a candle, and put it under a bushel, but on a candlestick: and giveth light unto all that are in the house. Let your light so shine before men, that they may see your good works, and glorify your father which is in heaven.

Matthew 5: 15 & 16

Day Eighteen Reflections

Daily Prayer: Chose this day to allow your light to shine by asking God to help others see your light.

How can your light shine?
_____
_____
_____
_____
_____

Have you ever been in darkness? (Explain)
_____

How do you see yourself?

From a scale of 0-100 what percentage would you rate yourself and why?

Day Nineteen

Thought of the day: Prayer changes things

Prayer: Communication with God.

The bible declares in Matthew 7:7 that "if you ask it shall be given to you". What you ask God for in prayer shall come to pass according to his will. Praying is how you express yourself to God and should be a big aspect of your daily life. It is not something you do when you need something or feel afraid. You need to pray through the good, bad, happy, or even sad. Having said that I say, God is always there in the good times and bad.

"All people can pray, because God is personal. However, sinners that have not trusted Jesus Christ for their salvation remain alienated from God. While unbelievers may pray, they do not have a rewarding fellowship with God. Which means they have not met the conditions according to the word for effective prayer ", according to nelsons student bible dictionary. Many people pray for particular things. Prayer is defective without having faith while praying. Praying with no faith is like sitting in a car and letting it run, which will not get anywhere. It does not matter how hard one is praying, if lack of faith is there, things will not happen the way that you want them. That means that you must work your faith.

People mess up attempting to tell God how things need to happen. God has everything planned the way that he needs. I am a firm believer in prayer. Now, let's not get things twisted. Pray for yourself and others as well.

Do not pray for bad things to happen to people, as this can be turned onto you. Sometimes when you pray for things, you want God to act right then. Remember this! He may not come when you need him the most, but for some reason he will always be on time.

Understand that he heard your prayers. He sees your tears. Late in the midnight hour, he was right there when no one else was. I do not know whom this is for, but somebody has been praying for quite some time now, and it seems as if your prayers are not being heard. God wanted me to speak to you by encouraging you that he has it.

See That You Are A True Inspiration

You have to let yourself go and cry out to him. Never stop believing what God can do in your life. Never stop praying. Never stop believing, when the odds are against you pray. Everyone including children and adults have the ability to pray. It does not matter what is said. Your conversation is between you and God.

How will you get to God? Let the Holy Spirit reign down. Prayer is a tool that helps you gain knowledge or understanding. Even Jesus prayed several times. By the power of prayer, lives change. People can be healed. One night the doctor said my father would not make it out of the hospital. I knew that at that moment I would have to pray. While my family were hurting and crying, I began praying because I knew that prayer is powerful.

Once God sees it and you give it to him you must allow him to handle it. Prayer has the power to change many things in your life for good and bad. Prayer can change a spouse, a child, an addict, the

True Inspiration

boss, or people that are in the workplace. You have an effective life. Therefore, you should have an effective prayer life.

What is better than prayer? Allow God to do his will first and furthermost. When God denies you that means what you prayed for did not line up to God's word. A key factor is to always stay prayed up.

Rejoice evermore. Pray without ceasing. In everything give thanks: for this is the will of God in Christ Jesus concerning you. 1 Thessalonians 5: 16-18

<u>Day Nineteen Reflections</u>

Daily Prayer: If you must want something from God then ask him for that very particular thing, but while you are praying don't forget to thank him of his wondrous works he has done in your life

Have you ever really prayed for something and was denied that very same thing?

_____
_____
_____
_____

See That You Are A True Inspiration

_____
_____

What are some things that you are currently praying for?

_____
_____
_____
_____
_____

How would you feel before you have prayed?

_____
_____
_____
_____
_____

What made the difference after you have prayed?

_____
_____
_____
_____
_____

See That You Are A True Inspiration

How will you become effective and powerful through prayer?

_____
_____
_____
_____
_____
_____

Day Twenty

Thought of the day: It is time to stop making excuses

Excuse: to say that one is not required to do something: granting exemption or release to: reasons as to why something cannot be done.

An excuse can come in the form of many different things. This is a dressed up lie that is told. Most of us needed an excuse for something at some point in our lives. First and furthermost please stop living every single day of life with an excuse. People who make excuses over nothing need to conduct a self-reality check. I never understand the reasons people make excuses. Excuses never matter. It is due to people being lazy and do not want to do what is expected of them. People will complain and make excuses on the job and other places. A person that always make excuses will never get anywhere, until he or she accepts some things about themselves. Before anything ever happens people will make an excuse. People use any excuse not to go in to work or even not to go to church. You will always find one person who is always using some sort of excuses. For example, have you ever had an appointment? You needed an excuse slip to get out of being tardy or absent. Excuses are generally used for the purpose of getting out of something that we don't want to do. People will not own up to their responsibilities due to immaturity still in their life. For this cause an excuse is made. The majority of us have been guilty of calling out of work. We make an excuse or claim that something drastic has happen. When in fact it never did. As you grow and learn you cannot live every day in a lie or an excuse. When the terminology "excuse me" is used it is a way of saying pardon me. If a parent continues to make excuses, then what is the child getting from that? You are teaching the child too quit, give up, or not do it. Before you know it the child will reflect you by making excuses in school, or home. The excuses should end here. Live your life without an excuse. That excuse pass is no longer needed. The excuse is the easy way out. We can make them at any point in our lives. Remember this key tip! Making an excuse for anything will cause you to fail and miss a blessing. If anything, it will slow you

See That You Are A True Inspiration

down from the thing(s) that God would have for you to do. It is time to stop making excuses, because they are pointless.

Then Moses said to the Lord, "Please, Lord, I have never been eloquent, neither recently nor in time past, nor since you have spoken to your servant; for I am slow of speech and slow of tongue. Exodus 4:10

<u>Day Twenty Reflections</u>

Daily Prayer: Simply pray by not excuses throughout the day

How can you prevent yourself from making excuses?
_____
_____
_____
_____
_____

Why do you believe you make excuses?
_____
_____
_____
_____

See That You Are A True Inspiration

Day Twenty One

Thought of the day: Just do it out of respect

Respect: to treat or deal with something that is good or valuable in a proper way: regard as being worthy of admiration, because of good qualities: a particular way of thinking about something or looking at something.

 Have you ever heard the saying "you don't have to like me, but you will respect me? " Most people don't understand the true meaning of respect. A lot of people in today's time demand respect. Respect is something that is never under demand. It is an act given. It is earned.
 As we grew up, we were taught to respect our elders. We were also taught to always be polite and use manners. It sad that the generation we live in has lost respect. Youth are to the point that they no longer care about respect.
 A lot of youth believe that carrying a gun and killing someone will earn them respect. In actuality it earns them nothing but a life sentence. Of course, no one wants to be disrespected. People have lost respect for themselves. It is hard for others to respect you

when you have no respect for yourself. It is even harder having respect for others when people don't respect themselves.

Most relationships or friendships fail due to lack of respect for each other. Now, allow me to say this, it's not safe to continue to take mess from others. This just means be tactful about the approach. We respect people such as clergy, policeman, firefighters, military personnel, etc. We respect them, due to their job or position of authority.

People will respect you or disrespect you whether they like you or not. So some may ask the question, how is it possible to respect someone who continues to disrespect me? It's all about character and integrity. It could also be based on attitude and approach. While others are disrespecting you remember that God always favors us.

Remember this! To be completely respectful one must do the following: **Recognize** the inherent worth of all people. **Eliminate** derogatory words from your vocabulary. **Speak** with people, not at them or about them when their back is turned. Also encourage someone and continue to speak positive. **Practice** empathy for yourself and others. Put yourself in others shoes for a while to really understand how they are feeling. **Earn it** by showing your worthy behaviors. **Consider** others and their feelings by what you do or even possibly say. **Treat** everyone the same way. It doesn't matter about their religion, race, or sex. Be consistent by your

See That You Are A True Inspiration

actions. Always be courteous. It is that simple. **R-E-S-P-E-C-T.**

Make today the day to show respect by not being disrespectful. Disrespect me to get disrespected is a horrible mentality to have. It doesn't work that way. I certainly believe everyone should get treated the way they treat you. It's just best to show kindness anyhow.

God created all people. He created us differently for many reasons and a purpose that we may not understand. Regardless, of how we perceive other people to be. They are God's creations, and it is God's will for us to show respect to everyone, despite the way they may treat us or what they may say to us. Remember this, respect and obey those that rule over us.

In all things shewing thyself a pattern of good works: in doctrine shewing un-corruptness, gravity, sincerity, sound speech, that cannot be condemned; that he that is of the contrary part may be ashamed, having no evil thing to say of you. Titus 2:7 – 8

<u>Day Twenty One Reflections</u>

Daily Prayer: It may seem hard to show respect to others who continually is disrespectful toward us;

See That You Are A True Inspiration

however you need to ask God to allow your heart be full of love and kindness toward others.

What do you believe the terminology "respect "means in your own words?
_____
_____
_____
_____
_____

Have you ever disrespected someone?
_____
_____
_____
_____
_____

How do you feel about respecting others more?
_____
_____
_____
_____
_____

Who are the main people in your life that you respect?

True Inspiration   *See That You Are A*

_____
_____
_____
_____
_____

Day Twenty- Two

Thought of the day: The joy of procrastination

Procrastination: to be slow or late about something that should be done: to delay something until a later time because you do want to do it, because you are lazy: putting something off intentionally and habitually

    The joy of procrastination. Yep, that is a joy. There is no joy in procrastination. We all are guilty of this. It's almost as if it comes natural to human beings to procrastinate. This is where the excuses will begin to start. Putting things off that may not seem important. Everything you do is important in your life some way or another. People will put things off and not get them done in a timely manner. By all means procrastination will most definitely get the best of you. For example, having an important assignment, but refusing to complete it. This is something that is a worst night- mare for us. I say that, because we will make procrastination a habitual thing of life. It is very detrimental to us. When one always procrastinates, they are telling themselves to simply fail. You should not want to live in a world full of procrastination. I can remember growing up and being asked to do something around the house. I would put it off by having the mindset of doing it later only to cause myself more grief by getting in trouble. Procrastination is what causes us more trouble. I really hate to say this, but people will even procrastinate on Christ. When it's time to go to church, people have in their mind that they will go next week or the week after. Eventually, they will stop going. When it's time to pray, we live by saying I will pray later. When it is time to fast, we have set our minds on fasting later. Procrastination will affect our daily endeavors. It is not good for our mind, nor is good for our body. This is a large part that reflects our perennial struggle with self- control, as well as our inability to accurately predict how we'll feel tomorrow, or the next day. Procrastinators may say they perform better under pressure. That's their way of justifying it to put things off. This will kill you in every single way. We all need to understand that we must stop our procrastination. Either that or it will consume you. This could be done far more quickly if you begin to put emphases on it, in order to begin to quit procrastination.

See That You Are A True Inspiration

> *The soul of the sluggard desires and hath nothing: but the soul of the diligent shall be made fat.*
> *Proverbs 13:4*

<u>Day Twenty- Two Reflections</u>

Daily Prayer

God has called you for a purpose. Simply ask him to allow procrastination to move out of your way.

How does procrastination stop people?
_____
_____
_____
_____
_____

What are ways you feel necessary to overpower procrastination?
_____
_____
_____
_____
_____

True Inspiration

Explain the things that you have procrastinated about_____
_____
_____
_____
_____
_____

Day Twenty- Three

Thought of the day: Do not get caught up with living in a lie.

Lie: Something said to be false: making an untrue statement with the intent to deceive: misleading impression.

    A good percentage of people have told some sort of lie throughout their lifetime. Even if it was a little white lie. Some may have told lies to cover something up as if it was never done in the first place. Lying is never the quality to have in the things we do.

See That You Are A True Inspiration

Relationships have failed due to lack of trust or people covering things up. People that have been lied on numerous of times will refuse to move into another relationship. That person has now became a victim of lies. That is all he or she knows. Before they know it, they are now telling lies because of someone that wanted to say something. Being involved with a liar is never any good for us. If you are involved with someone that is constantly lying to you then it is best that you find your way out that situation immediately. A liar is one of the biggest things that God hates. When a lie is told, another lie will have to cover up that one. Lying is known to be very dangerous. It sometimes will amaze me at the lies people will tell in order to get gratification for self-remedies. It sad to say that a liar will start to believe their own lies. One of the scariest things is a person who tells lies and believes them. One may even tell lies due to him or her not trusting himself or herself. They wrap themselves in lies because they are afraid of the truth or afraid of the consequences. Most people don't like the truth, because it is so powerful. The truth can do damage that can be recovered; however there is no fixing a lie once it is told. Lies can cost others who surround you so much damage. For example, one of my previous jobs as a Program Manager, someone lied on me and falsely accused me of something I had no part of. Because, of something said it cost me my job. This same very thing happened when I was in middle school. How is it that others will enjoy pleasures such as this? How do others feel when it has happened to them? You cannot get upset at the truth. A lot of people can handle a lie quicker than the truth. I say this because lies are all that some people will ever be able to fully comprehend. Their lifestyle is based on a lie. We often tell lies to avoid trouble. Lying is a horrible spirit to have. It is a lying demon that has the person's heart. Don't live in lies. Don't let something this detrimental ruin a blessing that God has in store for you. Change your mindset and stop the lies. Lies will get rumors started. Something that has no existence that others think is true. One wise man told me that you can steal my all, but the moment you lie, everything will be gone. Think about that for a second. I cannot elaborate on the fact that one simple lie can hurt or affect others who mean something dear to us. Lying has its ways of scarring others emotionally, spiritually, and mentally. I want you to get this in your mind. Despite, the lies that people have told, you still can manage to be a great conquer. People will also lie all the time. Especially, if they do not like you. Our closest friends, family, and coworkers can be the main one to lie on us. Yes it does hurt, but remember that Jesus said you are more than a conqueror. They even lied on Jesus for everything he was worth and everything that he had done. They also betrayed him. Betrayal is the one thing we feel when we are lied on. Sometimes the adversary will place lies in your head when God really wants you to do something or when God is moving you to a higher place. That is how the adversary will make every attempt to stop you. When one lives in lies they actually are afraid to see the truth within their heart. If you really want to get closer to God then stop lying. This is when you ask God to forgive you and to purge your heart. The devil has God's people telling lies, because he can't stand when God is revealing the truth. That is why problems exist in your home, on your job, in your relationships, or in your family. That's due to the devil persuading you of a lie. While God has revealed the truth, we allow flesh to get the way to blind our eyes of what God is trying to say.

Then said Jesus to those Jews which believed on him, if ye continue in my word, then are ye my disciples indeed; and ye shall know the truth, and truth shall make you free. John 8: 31- 32

Day Twenty- Three Reflections

Daily Prayer: You too can also come out of this horrible act. If you are a part of this first ask God to forgive, then you must repent, after which you must ask God to make you over completely by delivering you from this.

See That You Are A True Inspiration

How will you prevent lies from coming out of your mouth?

How can you prevent lies from entering your heart to overtake your spirit?

Have you ever been in a situation where you were falsely accused of something (explain)?

Have any lies ever changed your life?

True Inspiration   *See That You Are A*

_____
_____
_____
_____

Explain how a lie may affect others or change their life?

_____
_____
_____
_____
_____
_____

Day Twenty - Four

Thought of the day: Learn to be thankful.

Thankful: the aspect of praise that shows thanks for something: glad something has happened, that something or someone exists: expressing thanks: grateful.

See That You Are A True Inspiration

Are you thankful? Many of people will accept something, but they are not thankful for it. It is imperative that you learn to appreciate the smallest things in your life. I hate to say this, but a lot of people are very ungrateful. People will began to take the smallest things for granted. One of the most important things to learn is to be thankful. Be thankful for the good times and the bad times. It may sound strange; however it is true. The good and bad makes your character. One of the most valuable things that I have learned was that I need to become closer to my family. Sometimes they may only come around when they need something; however you still must be thankful. Sometimes people fail to give credit to God for all the things that he has done for us. People will appreciate you more when you appreciate them. It is as simple as appreciating the little things that someone has done for you. Your life can change by you becoming more appreciative. I look at how people take life for granted, but until something happens that's when they will become grateful. It's very saddening that something has to happen for people to be thankful. It's almost as if God has to wake you up to be appreciative. We live in a world where people take the smallest things for granted. As you will grow more, you become more thankful. It is never hard to show appreciation of something or someone most dear to you. So I would encourage you to be thankful. People will no longer want to do anything for you if you are not thankful. Every single day life is given to people, sometimes they fail to thank God for that day; which God should be our main priority. When one has finally became appreciative of things and people that are placed in their life he or she can finally say that they are thankful.

In everything give thanks: for this is the will of God in Christ Jesus. 1 Thessalonians 5:18

Day Twenty – Four Reflections

Daily Prayer: Today when you pray don't ask God for anything, simply thank him for something he has done for you.

What are some things you are thankful for?
_____
_____
_____
_____
_____

True Inspiration

Have you ever been ungrateful?

What helps you be more thankful?

Did God show you anything either by your gratefulness or ungratefulness?

Day Twenty - Five

Thought of the day: Being broken vs being rebuild

Broken: Bearing a burden, made weak, torn into pieces, damaged, hurt, smitten, wounded, scarred, or destroyed

Rebuild : renew, recover, fixing, putting things back together, make changes to, start over, build again, restore, or in the process of lifting up

    Broken can mean a variety of things. Whenever something is broken there is a rebuilding process behind it. For example, as a child did you ever break something in your mother's house? All of a sudden your mother grabs a tube of super glue. Then your mother will super glue the thing(s) that you broke back together. As time goes by, the thing that was broken now has to go through its process of reconstruction or healing. That is the way our life can be. You are broken at the moment, until God has to super glue you back together. You are wounded and torn open for the moment, until God has to fix you back together. I am sure most of you have been broken or some of you may be broken right now.

True Inspiration

Being broken is never easy. While you are going through the healing process remember this, God will certainly lift you up. Some people have been broken for so long that they have forgot the things that God can do. Never put yourself in a situation where you lose trust out on God. It doesn't matter about your struggle. It doesn't matter the circumstances, please don't lose your trust in God. This is when more problems will occur. Understand that nothing is too hard for God. The bible tells us in 1 Peter chapter 5:7 to cast all of our cares upon him; for he cares for us. That means God want us to tell him everything. All the hurt, pain, and guilt we should give it to God. Whatever the care is God has it. Hold up your head and encourage yourself. In spite of brokenness walk into God's favor. Allow him to surround you. Being broken creates a negative place for your mind and your spirit. It is time to get out of that negative place. Stop hiding behind the mask. People will see your smile on the outside, but they wouldn't understand that you are in so much turmoil. They would never understand what you were dealing with on the inside. People would never see your struggle. Having said that, you never allow people to see what you are in. Never give someone else the opportunity to see the mess that you are going through. Frankly, it is no one else's business of what you are in. Allow God to sustain you because he hasn't finished with molding you into who you need to be. Jesus was speaking with Jews according to John 2:18-21. Then Jesus told the

See That You Are A True Inspiration

Jews to destroy the temple. The Jews seemed very shock when he said this, because he said that he would rebuild it up in three days. Often times we find ourselves questioning the things that God can do. I have come to understand that God is God. I never need to question his works. I have seen the things that he can do. A lot of people could not walk in someone else's shoes for a day. Then people try to manipulate others at the stage of the broken process. It's not a matter of being a strong person. It's all where you may find strength. Strength is also something that allows us to recover. I do understand that the first stage of brokenness can destroy us mentally, emotionally, and spiritually. I would simply encourage others to really lean on God during hardships of life. God is always the healer. You need to quit doing things your way, because your way is the main way that will mess you up every time. Certain things as well as people, God will remove from a person's life. That something or someone has cause you to become distracted, so he has to remove these things out of your life only so he can finish what he started in you. This is a way he reveals himself to you. Now, I must say this. Quit giving the adversary so much room within your life. Sometimes the things we go through, the first person we blame it on is God or the enemy; however people will never understand that they were made to go through something. It is only to make us stronger and much better than before. In others words, God has it all for your better. If you can take it then you make it. Whatever you may be doing right now continue to do it. I say this because God has graced you with a gift and a perfect opportunity. Most people should understand that it is time to get back up. Stop allowing everything to get you down. In other words, God is saying to you that he will rebuild your broken temple.

For thou hast broken the yoke of his burden, and the staff of his shoulder, the rod of his oppressor, as in the day of Midian. Isaiah 9: 4

Day Twenty – Five Reflections

Daily Prayer: Use your strength to your best advantage. Open your heart up to God by praying that he will fix the things that have been broken in your life and the things that have broken you.

What things have broken you?
_____
_____
_____
_____
_____

True Inspiration

How were you able to heal or find strength in the midst of these things?

_____
_____
_____
_____
_____

Being broken has the tendency to change people. Explain how things changed you as a person?

_____
_____
_____
_____
_____

What are some things you learned during your broken?

_____
_____
_____
_____
_____

What things did you learn during the rebuilding process?

_____

Day Twenty - Six

Thought of the day: Going through the healing process

Healing: restoration of health; being spiritual recovered

When something has been broken it goes through its rebuilding process. During that rebuilding process it needs time to heal. For example, have you ever scraped your knee, or accidentally cut yourself. Now, take a look at that knee or the place that you have been cut. The mark is still there. Let's apply this to our daily lives in things we go through.

Some of you have been healed from whatever you were going through, but it left a mark. It left pain in your heart and it also caused some people to be traumatized. You are still bruised from the things that have been treacherous in your life; however God has declared that you have been healed from whatever it may be. When people think of the word heal they think of a miracle. God had the miracle already set.

See That You Are A True Inspiration

I can remember having a dream of my mother. In this dream I see her walking toward me. I have never seen this since I was in high school. Now, I just imagine my mother and father walking in heaven every single day.

Let's go back to when I prayed for both of my parents. Believe it not her and my father are healed. Sometimes we need to be healed in a physical sense only to move into the supernatural. Think about that for a moment.

During the healing process is when you are at your most vulnerable point in life. However, you will fail to realize that when you are healing from things. Healing gives the body time to recover from the things it has been put through. It will allow time for more growth and a better opportunity. Apply that to the spirit. Give it time to heal from what it has been placed through.

Not to mention, that the healing process of the spirit gives you time to think, cry, pray, and most of all get closer to God. Again, I say you must bring your flesh under subjection while your spirit is trying to heal. I found that out while healing from many things.

There are some things that you may still be healing from, but it got better. The adversary uses this as his most advantageous point over us. While going through the healing process you are weak, but when you come out you are stronger than ever before. So, give yourself time to heal spiritually, mentally, and emotionally.

After getting out of a bad relationship we need time to heal before jumping into another one. Eventually, your frustration goes out on the other person, which is never something good. Although, the healing process is a sluggish process, you must accept this for the best of yourself.

People should understand that this is a process to help you better yourself. It is not intended to harm you. It does help you to become a better person and closer to your loved ones.

The best thing to do while healing is to have a consistent prayer life. That also comes with continuously studying the word of God. These are the only ways of finding strength during the process of healing. Everyone needs time to heal. Whether it be in a relationship, in life, dealing with a loss, emotionally, or spiritually, the healing process is one good thing someone can experience, because during that time you are able to cope with many factors, as well as learn different things about yourself.

After going through a heart breaking or traumatic experience, it will change your focus. Always know that God is always your strength. An important factor is to always stay active. It doesn't matter how it is done just stay active. It helps with coping and keeps the mind off of certain things that you don't need to be thinking of. Do not let sickness, a bad relationship, or even something in life overtake

True Inspiration

you by destroying you. Even you can be healed and now it is time to be healed. As a matter of fact, it can no longer stop you, because you have been healed. I want to encourage you of going through the healing process with a positive mindset. The negative attitude will always kill your spirit. When things come against you the bible declares in Isaiah 54: 17 that no weapon formed against us shall prosper. That is the perfect way to truly heal. This is a way someone can value him or herself by truly healing.

But he was wounded for our transgressions, he was bruised for our iniquities: the chastisement of our peace was upon him; and with his stripes we are healed. Isaiah 53: 5

Day Twenty – Six Reflections

Daily Prayer: On today the things that you feel you need to be healed from call those things out in prayer.

In your own words what does it mean to really be healed?

_____
_____
_____
_____
_____

What are some things you need to be healed from?

_____
_____
_____
_____
_____

How can you apply this to your life?

_____
_____
_____
_____
_____

See That You Are A True Inspiration

Day Twenty-Seven

Thought of the day: Stop living in the past

Past: the events of a person's life, of place, etc.: having existed in a time before the present: from done, or used in an earlier time.

    It is 2015 and people are still living in things happening years ago. I can remember in school the teacher would explain something in past tense. Basically, past tense is something that had already happened through time. What is the reason that people continue to live in the past? I want you to understand that it is time to move on from the past. Stop allowing things that occurred throughout your life to still exist within your mind. People will dwell on the past until they die. The one thing that could be slowing you down is the past, because you are dwelling on something so much. You have a good past and a bad past. You cannot control the things that you have done. A lot of times people try to control the things that others have done to them. Then they try to assume revenge, which is never good. The past comes with experiences. The past also comes with growing and learning. Because, you had to learn from it in order to find happiness in the past. If it was a mistake, then do not pursuit after it any longer. It may be hard to let go of a traumatic experience. I truly understand that, however better yourself and better your life from it. I hear many stories of things that may have happened in someone's past. Now, we all have some sort of skeletons in the closet. Leave those dusty scary things wherever they may be. Become the person that God wants you to be. In other words focus on yourself, because you don't belong to your past, neither does it belong to you anymore. Having said that, do not live in any more sorrow. The journey has just began for you to move forward. Move to a higher calling, determination, and move to victory. Why would anyone ever let the things of the past have a superfluous amount over his or her life? Understand that living with the past will never get you anywhere in life. It is certain that the past can change the life of a person; however it's all in your ability of coming out of the past. That means to look beyond your past. Do not attempt to reconnect to the past. There are evil spirits in your past that want you back. Some people that were in your past may even want you back. A speaker by the name of Evangelist Betty Payne once spoke on letting the dead be dead (Matthew 8: 22). Things you go through happen for a reason. When it comes to relationships, some people are a season, while others are in your life for a reason. The seasonal

See That You Are A True Inspiration

folks are the ones who are just there periodically. They come and go like the weather. They are same people who teaches us a lesson .Whereas, the reasonable people better. They have made us better. The reasonable people are the ones who will always be there for you. Understand the two, because they both may be affiliated with your past. Your past is what tells your story because it will define who you were. It also defines character and attitude. Just because something happened in the past that we had no control over gives us no reason to blame it on God. Remember this! You have no control over the past, but you can control the things you allow in the future. Many people have done great things. Many of you have the potential to do great things, but you continue to look back at your past, which then will stop you from doing what you need to do. Take time to grow from things that may occurred in your life.

***Therefore if any man be in Christ he is a new creature: old things are passed away; behold, all things are become new.** 2 Corinthians 5:17*

<u>*Day Twenty- Seven Reflections*</u>

See That You Are A True Inspiration

Daily Prayer: Ask God to give you the ability to move forward.

What are some things you feel you are holding on?
_____
_____
_____
_____
_____
_____

How will you overcome the past?
_____
_____
_____
_____
_____
_____

How did the past affect you?
_____
_____
_____
_____
_____
_____

Read Matthew 8:22 and explain it in your own words_____
_____

See That You Are A True Inspiration

How does the past define you?

Day Twenty Eight

Thought of the day: Waste my anything, but do not waste my time

Time: something based on what one may doing in life: certain period of the day: lifetime: a nonspecial continuum that is measured through terms of events

which succeed one another from past through present to future.

      Time is all we have. Time is everything. Time is a limited resource. It is interesting. Everything revolves around time. Once it's gone, it will not come back. Bishop T. D Jakes said, "waste my anything, but don't waste my time". Time is very important in life. Most people live regretting the thing(s) that they should have done. Most people have the potential to go far; however they choose to waste time by doing nothing. Sometimes it's best to switch things up. Do not find yourself doing the same thing that you were doing yesterday, last week, several months ago, or even last year. Some people have become a sloth and everything that they attempted to do is slow. Some people are even slow for Christ. People will get up to be at work early, but they are either always late for Christ or will not stay in church longer than ten minutes. Here is an important tip! You can want something, and not pursue after it, which then causes a waste of time. I have learned that sometimes we begin to get in relationships to stay there for quite some time; however we are getting nothing out of it. When you become accustomed to doing the same thing, you have then allowed time to consume you. A lot of people spend time courting the wrong people. We spend time letting the wrong things and people get the best of us. Most marriages end up in divorce, due to people rushing God's timing. When we may think we "love" someone, and God says this is not the one that I have predestined for you. Remember I spoke that God has the ability to speed up time or slow it down. My divorce was a year that was a waste of time. I could have been doing something better with my time. It is so true that time does fly. Everything happens quicker then we think. I have learned that some people will not use their time wisely. Bishop T. D is my role model and I remember when he said, "I would hate to die and not do the thing I was born to do". See we are born with a purpose. It is sad that some of you will not walk into your purpose. God gives you something, but you will turn the other way. I have questioned several times what could I have done better? See this is the one question that no one never wants to ask themselves. Do what you can now while you still have the time. Time and procrastination are two things that can cause grief. Remember this, once something is done you cannot get it back. It saddens me that a lot of people spend time playing with their life instead of trying be better. Life is full of eventful things. Sometimes we can spend so much time on other things and forget to spend time on us. It's now time to spend your time building your life and your future. It is only a matter of time. Please don't spend life wasting your time. There are many great things to do. Stop wasting time doing nothing. Quit allowing life to go by.

See That You Are A True Inspiration

See then that ye walk circumspectly, not as fools, but as wise, redeeming the time, because the days are evil. Wherefore be ye not unwise, but understanding what the will of the Lord is. Ephesians 5: 15-17

<u>*Day Twenty Eight Reflections*</u>

Daily Prayer: Ask God to help you with things you feel that are time consuming so that you are not wasting your time on the wrong things.

How do you use your time?
_____
_____
_____
_____
_____

What could you do better for you?
_____
_____
_____
_____
_____

In due time what are some things that you want to do?

True Inspiration   See That You Are A

_____
_____
_____

What areas of life do you feel have been wasted?_____
_____
_____
_____
_____

_____

Day Twenty - Nine

Thought of the day: Quit being selfish

Selfish: having showing concern only for yourself and not for the needs or feelings of other people: egoistic

    Have you ever been told it is not good to be selfish? Some of you have even been told to share, or that sharing in caring. As a little child growing up, I was always taught to share. It didn't matter if they gave it back or not. Most selfish people only think about themselves because they are not willing to please others. In others words they are care free about their actions or words. These same people will take

See That You Are A True Inspiration

family for granted, leave their friends or care less about their relationship/ spouse. A selfish person is never a good person. They are always arrogant. They are selfish, because they haven't learned the importance of humility. A person that is always selfish could be the most dangerous person to always be around. When a person becomes selfish they have become spoiled. They want someone to always appease them, but you will never get anything in return. They always want something and they will never help you. If someone is selfish, then that person should consider some heart searching with themselves. "Well you can't blame me for the way I am", some may say. Yes, you are right, I cannot blame you for the person that you are, so that means that you blame yourself for the way that you are. These same people allow **PRIDE** to destroy their character. A lot of times these same people will care less about what you have to say. Most of all, I am sure they will not care what God has to say. Selfish people have the most problems in their life. Although, they think that they don't due to them being so care- free. Everything is about their own self-gratification. They seek pleasures in self along with the world. They can also be classified as drama starters. Selfish people love seeing others struggle because they love talking about others. Most of the time they are easy to spot. They think that the entire world revolves around them. Some people may even go far enough to think that they are God. It is best to allow God to deal with them. Why are people selfish? It could be the way that they were raised or something behind their childhood that has happened to them. I never understood the reason that people love themselves that much. It is to the point where they must be selfish toward others. People are selfish due to them not being able to really value themselves. Most selfish people don't know how to get things done, because there is not a care in the world. In fact, it is always better to give then to receive. There is no real way to really deal with a selfish person. Selfish people are those that love holding on to things, which causes them to be greedy. In other words they have something to where they don't value others and their opinion. Another thing of selfishness is the fact that they have less going for themselves. They are not willing to compromise or give up their time. If you want to know who your true friends are then ask them for something and wait for the response that you will get. Family is guilty of being selfish as well. See I find it interesting when people need me one day, but when I need them they are no-where to be found. I say that, because selfish people are so quick to try to manipulate others.

Through desire a man having separated himself, seekers and in termed let with all wisdom. Proverbs 18:1

Day Twenty – Nine Reflections

See That You Are A
True Inspiration

Daily Prayer: On today ask God to give you something that can be returned to others by you not being selfish.

In your words explain selfishness
_____
_____
_____
_____
_____
_____

Have you ever been selfish?
_____
_____
_____
_____
_____
_____

What is your reaction toward a selfish person?_____
_____
_____
_____
_____
_____
___

See That You Are A
True Inspiration

If you were ever selfish, how would you make plans to stop being selfish?

_____
_____
_____
_____

What do you think may cause a person to become selfish?

_____
_____
_____
_____
_____

<u>Day Thirty</u>

Thought of the day: The pursuit of happiness

Happiness: the state of being happy: an experience that makes you happy

See That You Are A True Inspiration

Happiness is something everyone wants. It could be on the job, in life, in an education, or in a relationship. The key to happiness is you. This is one thing that really defines you. If no one else will make you happy, then make yourself happy. Stop living in a phase of depression. Stress and depression are things you don't need in your life. Most people will sit and wait for happiness, while others will go chasing after it. Some people don't even know how to get happiness, while others do not know the true meaning of happiness. When you become unhappy in a relationship, the best thing to do is get out of it. It will never do you any good sitting around trying to figure out the reason that you are not happy. Talk about a waste of time. Happiness is something that will come naturally. A lot of people don't know their level of happiness. It is even worse that they cannot get there. People want to be happy in all the things that they do. Sometimes the wrong things and people can take that away. Far too many of us allow others to steal our happiness. This would make someone confused on their true happiness. I once was asked the question, " if God wants me to be happy, then why are there so many difficulties in my life"? Every now and then you need some difficulties to allow you to see yourself. This gives you the opportunity to see your true happiness. What could be the reason that people are so evil? God didn't create anyone to wake up evil every single day. An important trait that will always make us happy is knowing that we are loved. I mean the feeling of knowing we are really loved. This gives you the opportunity to love yourself even more. If he or she is doing everything to make you happy and you still cannot be happy then something is not right. Have you ever thought that you could be the problem? A lot of times people don't see that they are the ones causing more problems. Why do people stay in mess trying to figure things out? Think of it this way, when you as a person can look at someone or begin to think of that person and began to smile, this defines true happiness. Another factor to happiness is doing the things that you love. Some people love to write books, travel, exercise, etc. Whatever the things that make you happy are, continue to do them. Embrace the things of happiness. Success is another key of happiness. Everyone gets that wonderful feeling when something has been accomplished. After we have striven really hard for something, we know that we can do anything. Happiness along with success is a key combination to greatness. Never should anyone live in any type of unhappiness. God is too wonderful for you to live in stress, depression, or unhappiness. These are things that will begin to cause health issues. They can kills us literally. The last thing everyone wants is happiness in is finances. It may be hard to smile when bills are always due, and you have no money. Look at this way! You still have a roof, water, electric, or whatever have you. Some people have created a horrible environment for themselves.

See That You Are A True Inspiration

Although, we may be in debit at the moment, God wants to pull us out of it so our lifestyle is glorious. To those who are stressed and depressed every day, understand that God created you to smile. This means look at yourself in the mirror and appreciate the things you have by smiling at yourself. You are too blessed to be stressed. Evaluate the pursuit of your happiness. Turn everything into happiness.

In the day of prosperity be joyful, but in the day of adversity consider: God also hath set the one over against the other, to end that man should find nothing after him.

Ecclesiastes 7:14

Day Thirty Reflections

Daily Prayer: Ask God to help you find happiness in the things that you do or in certain people.

How can someone be happy?

See That You Are A True Inspiration

Explain your level of happiness

How will happiness effect your daily activities?

How does happiness effect your attitude?

See That You Are A True Inspiration

What are things that make you happy?

_____
_____
_____
_____
_____

Day Thirty-One

Thought of the day: where do you find strength?

Strength: the ability to resist being moved or broken by a force: quality of being strong.

Strength is something that means a lot. It is a way a defining a person's character, development, and growth in particular areas of life. This could also be a trait of something that makes someone special. Strength does come in many forms and in many ways that could change upon the situation. Strength is one of the things that can give us courage to do what is right when no one else will. It is known as the ability to cover all weakness.

See That You Are A True Inspiration

For example, have you ever been to a gym to work out? Next, there is this big huge person. It took time for him / her to get that way. Allow me to say this, after we have been through hell it takes time to gain strength. You have to start out slow in order to be so powerful. The more strength that a person has makes it the better for them.

Weakness will no longer be a factor due to strength covering all weakness. Your strength is giving you power. Despite, that you are weak at first, strength is what makes you stronger. People now will attempt to find strength in the wrong things and in the wrong people. A man cannot find strength through money, cars, clothes, drugs, alcohol, lust, or whatever else. If you think about it, after you have done the following, the problem still exist.

The best possible way to find strength is through God. Despite, your emotions, God is always the best answer. Strength in the spiritual matter comes by becoming closer to God, praying daily, fasting, and studying the bible. I have been asked the question, how are you so strong after all the hell that has come your way? Sometimes I ask myself that very same question. Believe me, it was never easy. My response to that question is always, "because, I know that I have God". I honestly don't know where I would be without God. My strength never came from me. I knew that I had help. Someone had to help me lift this weight off of my shoulders.

A person would never understand their strength until it is challenged. It is almost like faith. A person will never know the amount of faith that he/she may possibly have until it is challenged. Just like faith, you must work your strength. Everyone wants you to be strong, but they don't understand. I hear people sometimes telling others not to cry, however sometimes it is good to cry. It makes you stronger. Everyone has weak areas that they need to work on. This could pertain to a relationship, work, your studies, church, family, friends, or life.

See That You Are A True Inspiration

The strong areas suit you best because everyone has strength. The characteristics of a strong person allows them to see their weak areas. A strong person has endured a lot and they still find the strength to move on or let go. A bad experience or adversity does allow a person to become stronger due to the teaching in that. This is the one area of focus that gives you the ability to move on.

Strength does give a person power over certain things in his/ her life. However, it will not make a person dominant. When I use the word dominant it is referred to as being in control. Dominant can over power everything else. Sometimes it best to hit the brakes to stop having so much control. It's good to have control over your life because strength does not control the life of others. Strength is not an overpowering or ruling matter. Strength is the one thing that we all want to gain.

Do not allow certain things or people to make you weak. Life does come with challenges that you must face every day. Find your strength by moving forward and continue to pray until something happens, despite the pain, although it seems like there is no more left for you to take. It may even become hard to make it to your next phase. Find your strength, God had created you for a purpose that was never intended for you to give up. Some people will allow weakness to stop them. If there is no pain every once in a while then there is no gaining strength. When you become weak, you should allow God to lift you up. God is lifting you up every single time; which causes you to have a superfluous amount of strength. Now, it's time to get big and gain your strength back that will carry you over your weakness. You haven't pushed hard enough to gain power. You haven't prayed hard enough. That is the reason that the adversary continues to persuade you. Have you challenged yourself? Have you motivated yourself? The most important thing of strength is learning to be

True Inspiration

strong. That means grow stronger in God first and all extracurricular activities second.

I can do all things through Christ which strentheneth me

Philippians 4:13

Day Thirty-One Reflections

Daily Prayer: On this day it is important that we identify our weak areas whatever they may be in, and ask God to touch our lives by giving us the strength we need to continue to make it as well helping us grow in our weak areas. Also ask God that he will help you grow stronger in him.

What are some qualities you have that may define your strength?

_____
_____
_____
_____
_____

What areas are you weak in?

_____

See That You Are A
True Inspiration

_____
_____
_____
_____
_____

What have you done to prove yourself?

_____
_____
_____
_____
_____

How will you become stronger in God?

_____
_____
_____
_____
_____

Day Thirty - Two

Thought of the day: Take the limits off

Limits: a point beyond which is impossible to go; boundary; extent; confinement; exasperating or intolerable.

See That You Are A True Inspiration

Is it safe to say that most people will limit themselves on what they can do? People will also put limits on the things that God can do. Please never limit God, as well as limiting yourself. God shall never count us out. An example of a limit may be driving down the interstate and things began to slow down. Something has happened that you cannot quite see at the moment. While you are taking the limits off, God has begun to place you under construction. You are able to move into greatness by being under construction. If a person wants to be called into greatness then he or must work the faith.

It is very imperative that you adhere to what God is telling you during this process. Two key ingredients of taking limits off are forgiveness and faith. Without faith your works are dead. While unforgiveness is in the heart it would be very hard to move. You should never allow anything to get in the way of getting to God. The story of the lady with the issue of blood reminds me of taking the limits off. It didn't matter that anyone would be in her way. She knew that she had to get to Jesus. Despite, the things that the adversary tried to do. Although, doctors tried to sign her off. She would still find a way to God. Another lady that reminds me of taking the limits off would be my mother and grandmother. You would never understand how these women were so sick, but they still pressed their way to church. This was their way of saying I must get to Jesus. I can't allow sickness to stop me or people to get in my way. Despite, the hurt and pain they may had been dealing with, they still would press on anyhow.

The problem is that pressing is not a factor. You have no excuse to allow things to get in the way of your break- through, miracle, healing, or deliverance. There are some things and people whom you must exclude out of your life. They all want to stop you by destroying you the best way that they may know how to do it. It is time to leave the bad habit(s). Leave the drugs and the addiction alone.

True Inspiration

The important factor is to focus on yourself. Before you can do anything (that includes getting into a relationship, going back to school, etc.) you must take time to focus on yourself. Understand that with God all things are possible. We as people also need to quit bucking at God. While taking limits off, it is important that you bring your flesh under subjection. You must overpower it by not allowing it to overpower you. When the flesh is weak, God will renew your strength. I never understood the reason that people will remove certain things out of their life only to turn back to it.

Get away from negative people and their negative words. Allow God to speak to your heart, as well as the mind. So how do I take the limits off? There are many ways that limits can come off. Compare limits to shackles. You are free once they come off. Remember this! A negative mindset will always equal a negative future. When you tell yourself that you can't, you've placed thoughts in your mind that will not allow you to complete the task. A lot of people have been fed up with many things. The weight of the world has been placed on our shoulders. Some may say that they are in so much mess and they need God just to see about them. Where is God when you need him? Lord you said that you wouldn't put more on me than I can bare, but this is too much for me. Although, you can't see him, you can feel his presence.

    Don't expect to break the cycle if you are unable to break the limits. Some of you are still living in fear. Some may still be living in mess. This means that we need God to help us. I would encourage you to encourage yourself. If God is for us, then who is more in the world that can stand against us? Who shall stand in our way if God is for us? Nothing or no one can stand over you. Sometimes we worry or fear that we may be defeated. Depression or stress get in our way as well. I understand that you may go to church every Sunday looking for a miracle or a break-though and it has yet to happen. Sometimes people go to church so heavy and leave out the same way. Your supposed find your break- through, deliverance, healing, anointing, and strength in this.

You need to spend more time praying. Limits are compared to obstacles. These obstacles are things that you step over. This is the main reason that you should move closer to God. Speak to the limits. Sickness you can't stay here. Depression it is time that you leave. Cancer you must go right now. Poverty I am pleading the blood. Tell your limits that you have God. Declare them to move. Stop allowing the limits to stand over you. You need to plead the blood over everything that is a hindrance. Making mistakes only means you are human; however still take your limits off.

The devil tried to mess with God's people because he wanted to distract us. The devil even tried to kill, steal, and destroy. Have you ever been on your job and the boss walks in? The atmosphere will begin to change. When the boss steps in the devil has to back up. He had to get his hands off of God's people. He had to take his hands off our children, finances, job, family, or church. As a matter of fact, it is time to take back everything that the adversary stole from God's people. So how are you going to get it back? You must continue to understand that God is great and that he will do exceedingly, abundantly, and certainly above all that you can ask for or think. It is also important to allow God to really finish what he started.

There are no limits. You are your only limit. It is time that you quit limiting yourself on your dreams, visions, or goals. So while folks are saying that you are no good, God is fixing you up. While folks are saying that you won't make it, he is cleansing you off. Everything that haters or the adversary attempted to do, remind them that they are giving you something good. Allow me to explain for a second. Romans 8: 28 says, "and we know that all things work together for the good of them that love the Lord according to his purpose". This means while the devil is causing mess in your home, at work, in school, or where ever. God is already preparing the good out it. GOD HAS FIXED IT; THEREFORE LET IT GO. People are at the period in life where limits are coming off. Some things are get ready to break. The release is on the way. That means you are getting ready for a breakthrough, because you are about to break through. Continue to press toward God by pressing toward the high mark. Quit looking at the past. As a matter of fact, quit looking at the situation. It is time to take the limits off. As Bishop Paul Morton would say, "The best is yet to come". Again, I say get away from the negative things and people that are causing a distraction.

Likewise the Spirit also helpeth our infirmities: for we know not what we should pray for as we ought: but the Spirit itself maketh intercession for us with groanings which cannot be uttered.
Romans 8:26

Day Thirty-Two Reflections

Daily Prayer: Ask God to remove anything or anyone who is hindering you from doing his will so that you become closer to God.

What are your limits?

How can you take the limits off?

What are some things that could be done better?

True Inspiration   *See That You Are A*

_____
_____
_____

How are you moving forward?

_____
_____
_____
_____
_____

What is your destiny?

_____
_____
_____
_____
_____

<u>Day Thirty - Three</u>

Thought of the day: Have some self-control

Self - Control: restraint or discipline exercised over one's behavior: the ability to control one's emotions, desires, feelings, or impulses

It starts with self. It is a reason that it is called self-control. People live everyday learning to control themselves, while others are still learning to control themselves. Understand that no one in this world is perfect; however there are certain things that we must learn to control. It is important to control yourself in a particular environment. Control your body, heart, soul, and mind. Everything will start to feed off the mind. Sometimes you can allow other people to have power over you. This gives them the opportunity to control you. One of the biggest things of maturity is having self-control. I certainly can attest to us having things we must work on. The thing that I never understand is people that have horrible attitudes for no apparent reason at all. It is hard to earn someone's trust and respect if you cannot have self-control. It is totally understandable that people love to be in control; however it is important to control your attitude and what you say. The things you say or do cannot be taken back once it is done. Your attitude is based on your reaction. People with lack of self-control cannot work well with others. They cannot respond well in an intense situation. I look at police officers, firefighters, EMT's, the military, and doctors. These people are highly trained to respond under intense situations. They must have the ability to think rationally, be skillful, and expeditious. They also must keep themselves under control. Sometimes it best to put our feelings aside for the moment. Some people have all the credentials, but have the wrong response. Sometimes you have to make yourself deal with the attitude of someone else. If you want to see others get even angrier keep yourself calm and watch how fast they blow up. Eventually, they will shut down. People are quick to act out due them having no control over themselves. Self-control is similar to humility. When you have self-control the ability to see things comes natural. Remember this! You have power over everything that concerns you. It is all based on your attitude toward others. It can also be something that is within your spirit. Having patience

True Inspiration

in a lot of areas could give you more self-control. It is important to be slow to anger and anything foolish.

A violent man enticeth his neighbour, and leadeth him into the way that is not good.

Proverbs 16: 29

Day Thirty-Three Reflections

Daily Prayer: On today it is important to learn to have self-control. Ask God to help you control your attitude

How should you learn to control yourself?

_____
_____
_____
_____
_____
_____

What are things that give you self-control?

_____
_____
_____

See That You Are A True Inspiration

Day Thirty-Four

Thought of the day: Stop allowing others to have your happiness

    As we previously discussed happiness four days ago, we will touch a little bit more on it but in a different sense. Now, let's start by saying it is good to be a kind hearten person; however it's the kind hearten people that get taken advantage of the most. We do more than we should for people and still get nothing. Quit allowing others to steal things that God has blessed you with. These things may be joy, happiness, love, kindness, goodness, faithfulness, gentleness and self-control. If you notice these are the fruits of the spirit. Never allow people so deep in your life that they start to control you.
    You can give someone your all, but it still not feasible unto them. People that are closest to you will always try to steal your happiness. They try to put you down by talking about you. They also think that they are in a position of dictatorship. They may do these things, because they never want to see you

True Inspiration

happy. I encourage you to stop giving people room to take advantage of you. If you cannot speak up, then they will continue to mistreat you. People are quick to back stab you. They will even act in a spiteful manner. They will smile in your face only to smile in the face of others about you. They will love you once only to hate you forever.

You can be a blessing to them, but they get the wrong perception of you. They are not happy; therefore they cannot stand seeing others happy. The bible tells us in Matthew 5:43-45 that we must love the ones who despise us; therefore you must learn to pray for these people. It is almost like a second nature. Please stop worrying about what people say or do. People will do anything to try to stop your blessing. Some people will mistreat others due to them having hatred in their heart or they are jealous. These people are known as haters. They can't find happiness in themselves due to them wanting the things that you have. They may not mean any harm, but in actuality they are doing more harm then they think. As a child of a king they shouldn't want to mess with us, because we are children of the King this gives them an even greater opportunity to continue to try and harm us. How is it possible for someone to continue to mistreat others? It makes not a bit of sense to me; anyhow people done these things to Jesus. They talked about him, lied on him, betrayed him, etc. Just to name a few. It is never good to cause yourself stress over nothing that even matters. I will say

True Inspiration

whatever you are doing keep doing it, because it is good. When God had created things into the world he had said, "it was good". Despite what people said or done, God noted that everything was good.

And whatsoever ye do, do it heartily, as to the Lord, and not unto men; knowing that of the Lord ye shall receive the reward of the inheritance: for ye serve the Lord Christ.

Colossians 3: 23-24

<u>Day Thirty-Four Reflections</u>

Daily Prayer: Ask God to cover you that no one is able to steal anything from you

Why would you allow others to steal your happiness?

_____
_____
_____
_____
_____

What are things you can do in order to not allow people that much room?

_____

True Inspiration   *See That You Are A*

_____
_____
_____
_____

Explain a time that you allowed someone to steal your hapiness_____
_____
_____
_____
_____

Day Thirty-Five

Thought of the day: Sometimes we take more things for granted

Taken for granted: an act of being unappreciative toward something or someone.

Granted means a variety of different things.

This is a different type of granted that we will talk

See That You Are A True Inspiration

about in this section. Have you ever taken things for granted and never realized that you were doing that? This is something we all have become guilty of at one point in our lives. Either we have taken others for granted or others have taken us for granted. When someone or something is being taken for granted, the value has been underestimated.

Sometimes God will bless us with many different things, but we choose take him and his blessing for granted at times. We ask God for things such as a great spouse, a car, a job, etc. Instead of really cherishing these things, we will leave them and take them for granted. The things that are taken for granted more on a spiritual level are Gods love, blessings, forgiveness, life, spiritual understanding and Jesus. Things must happen in order for us to appreciate what is given to us. We will attempt to get the things back, because we loved them so much. Just as God can bless you with something great, he can take it away from you. People have placed in their mind that they no longer care about what it may be.

Remember this! Once it's gone there is no coming back. Sometimes people will not know how to appreciate the small things that they have. It's even sad to say that people want to abuse, misuse, or run over the people that God has placed in their lives. Why would anyone want to wreck God's many blessings that he has restored upon them? This is something that can be done accidental or purposeful. It is done accidental, because people may not know that they are doing such a thing. It is done purposeful, because they know exactly what they are doing without a feeling of remorse, guilt, or shame. Sometimes you can take your own family for granted. It's sad that some people wouldn't want to appreciate what they have because they want better. They don't realize that God had given them something better. He gives us the best blessings of his own.

See That You Are A True Inspiration

Sometimes people feel the need to be stubborn. God gives you more each day that he allows you to live. So why is it hard for us to give him more? God sent Jesus to die for us, so we can return the favor by allowing God in our life and in our heart. Instead, we choose not to. This is an example that we take God our savior for granted more than we should. Sometimes we don't pray like we should. Sometimes we don't fast enough or obtain enough spiritual knowledge in the bible. Some people or things will never be appreciated; which is a horrible feeling. Relationships fail each day due to one feeling like he / she is being taken for granted.

A person cannot grow spiritually with the intent of taking others for granted. Being misunderstood is another reason that people get taken advantage of. Others have lived a horrible life or just got out of a horrible relationship, so they feel the need to take others for granted, because it was done to them. I strongly encourage you to let someone on today know that you love them and you are thinking about them. Thank someone in your circle. Things are happening that you have no control over, so it is good to encourage someone. No one likes the feeling of being taken advantage of. I can say that being taken for granted has really made me appreciate things and people more. It has also made me appreciate that someone special in my life more. It also helps us loves others in a more affectionate way. After one has been taken for granted he or she will learn to accept or see things in a different way.

Being taken for granted doesn't just happen within a relationship or family. It also happens on the job or even in church. It doesn't matter the time of day that it may happen. If people wanted to take advantage of others, then they would do it. They wouldn't care about your feelings or the location that it has taken place. It's hard to smile when you are taken for granted. It's hard to press on or move forward when you are taken for granted. It is hard to love someone else after we have been taken for granted in a past relationship. I never will forget having this conversation with my sister. I told her that I could never love anyone else again. I had also mentioned to her that my heart will be closed. This happened only for her to say, "Quan you should not do that, although you have been taken for granted, what will happen when you find that special someone?" Are you going to continue to be that way"? The problem that I had going through a divorce was the fact that I felt unappreciated. I done everything and still felt unappreciated. Knowing that I felt unappreciated, I could not focus on trying to make things better for myself. The best thing to do is to always apologize. Some people will take others for granted and never apologize. In others words they try to make you look like the bad person. Remember this! If you allow it to continue then it will continue. For some people, the biggest mistake is allowing the wrong people in their lives for far too long. Look at this way! There comes a time when you must say enough is enough. There is no playing the victim role when we are being honest.

Recompense to no man evil for evil. Provide things honest in the sight of all men. If it be possible, as much as lieth in you, live peaceably with all men. Dearly beloved, avenge not yourselves, but rather give place unto wrath: for it is written, vengeance is mine; I will repay, saith the Lord.

Romans 12: 17- 19

Day Thirty-Five Reflections

Daily Prayer: Despite whatever people have done to you or whatever you may have to others. Ask God for forgives over you or them and that he will allow you grace and mercy to press on toward many blessings that are in store you without holding a grudge.

How have you handled being taken for granted?
_____
_____
_____

See That You Are A True Inspiration

Have you prayed for certain people in your life?

What are somethings you would change after being taken for granted?

After being taken for granted, how would that help you improve your relationship with God, family, church, or relationship?

True Inspiration   *See That You Are A*

<u>Day Thirty- Six</u>

Thought of the day: Some people are so careless

Careless: not being careful: done, made, or said without enough thought or attention

Have you ever been in the car with a careless person? They fail to care about their actions while in car. They also fail to obey the laws. These people also fail to care about their life or yours. Imagine that being close to or with a careless person. Like a selfish person, they have no care. When becoming close or being in a relationship with a careless person, we are putting our lives in jeopardy. These are the most dangerous people to ever try to put up with. Some may say it's nice to be care- free. In fact it may be; however we should learn what to be care-free about.

    One of the best ways to cause grief is to worry about the small things. Depression can sneak upon us if we care of something as small as a penny. Some people have that care- free attitude, but it has affected them tremendously. Having the care-free attitude will affect the way people will see things in life, as well as the way people look at you. The care free attitude rules that person. It has control over the mind. Not to mention, it also affects the attitude daily. Attitude is something that is very important. Attitude is what gives others the first impression of us. That can be a negative or positive image of someone. It's bad to be careless while on the job, in any type of relationship, home, education, or future endeavors. Here is a tip! Careless people should take time to care, instead of putting other things before the issue. Although, some things may seem small for them, it could be a main concern for others. This means if they are close to others, they should at least take try to care second.

There could be many reasons that people no longer care. One could be others not caring for them. Another reason could be something they have seen in their child hood. They would care less of our emotions and expressions. A careless person will say how they care about church, family, friends, or relationships. Although, they may claim this, it would not be true. Compare this to a selfish person. Both in which are dangerous to ever be around. No one wants to be in a relationship where their needs are not met, or even worse where they feel they are not loved. We all want our feelings to be cared about. No it is not being "too sensitive". It is called being human. God created us with feelings and emotions to express ourselves. Our words and actions will always matter. They will always follow us. It could possibly affect others. Again, I say some people don't even care about their family.

They will do things to break or destroy their family. The main things that will destroy are family will be smoking, drinking alcohol, drugs, lust, and addictions. Its bad when these things are performed in front of children or while their kids are in the house. How careless can one be to do those kinds of things around their children? This means

See That You Are A True Inspiration

be **CAREFUL** of the ones you may entrust your life to. The mentality of a careless person will never understand the logic of a person who actually cares for him or her. This may be something he/ she has never had before. They could also be wresting with themselves or wrestling with their spirit. Again, they are selfish due to them not caring about their life. They may not care about their health, lifestyle, or body. God reminds in 1 Corinthians 6:19 to be careful of things that we do to our bodies, because it is a living temple of the most high. Sometimes we make careless decisions by not even knowing it.

For we ourselves also were sometimes foolish, disobedient, deceived, serving diver's lusts and pleasures, living in malice and envy, hateful, and hating one another. But after that the kindness and love of God our Savior toward man appeared. Titus 3:3- 4

<u>Day Thirty- Six Reflections</u>

Daily Prayer: Simply pray over your careless decisions that you made. Also pray for someone in your life that may be living a careless lifestyle and ask God to help him / her.

Why do people become careless?
___
___
___
___
___
___

In your own words explain "careless"
___
___
___
___
___
___

Have you ever been careless toward anyone in your life (family, significant other, friends, co-workers, etc.)?
___
___
___
___

True Inspiration   *See That You Are A*

_____

_____

What is the difference between a selfish person and a careless person?

_____

_____

_____

_____

_____

Day Thirty - Seven

Thought of the day: We are in a spiritual warfare

Warfare: Fighting against things that are trying to stop the spirit.

This is something that we all should know. Not to mention this is the one thing that we must pay attention to. A spiritual warfare is the one thing we deal with every day. These are things that try to stop your spirit. Not to mention that it will keep your spirit. It may also try to pull you away from God. These things can include the world, flesh, the adversary, or invisible foes. We conquer over these things by God's word, God armor, having faith, and the promises that Christ has given unto us. Our flesh can pull us away from God. Our past could even pull us away from God if we allow it to.

A solider is someone who must be covered in armor and ready for battle at all times. He must also be on alert. As a solider of God we must pray without ceasing, fast, endure hardness, be self-controlled, be on the alert, and most all cover ourselves from whatever the spiritual warfare may be. We have to guide our spirit every day. Spiritual warfare's can control us. For example, when soldiers go to combat they are always ready. They have all their equipment ready. Our best defensive tact is what the bible says. We must learn to stand on the word of God. God is our rock. The foundation that we must stand on is the bible. Spiritual warfare's come by the adversary not getting his way, which we should never allow him to have his way. Understand the haters or the adversary cannot stop you, until you allow them to do so. The

See That You Are A True Inspiration

adversary must go through God first in order to get to you. The adversary brings the temptation; however we must understand that the adversary will continue to kill, destroy, and steal from you. He wants to kill you spiritually. All the hardships we go through in life are to build us.

The adversary wants to see God's people depressed, stressed and not blessed. He does these things, because he doesn't like the things GOD has done for us. The key is to break the spiritual warfare. Break those things meaning no good. Break the addiction, depression, and break the cycle. You have many things that want to destroy you; however it will not. I declare that right at this moment. The devil has to get away from you. You are too gifted and anointed to deal with a spiritual warfare. There are some things that wanted to kill some people; however God would not allow it. As Donnie McClurkin said, "we fall down, but we get up". In fact we do fall down, but we must learn to ask God for forgiveness or even repent if that is the case. This is the way that we can pick ourselves back up again. If you give the adversary room to steal your spirit or your fruit (love, joy, peace, or faith) then he will do just that. Evil spirits are literally fighting against you. They know that you are powerful, so they are prepared to hit you where it hurts you the most.

A child of God must know how to deal with these things. Spiritual warfare's come when you are at your weakest point. Understand that what makes you stronger is having GOD. That means that you must learn to get closer to God during these times. Continue to feed the spirit with good things. Never allow the spirit to die. Do not allow the spirit to get under any attack. When your flesh is weak allow God to renew your strength. Always be covered and always keep your weapon (the word of God) in your heart. Control your flesh. Isaiah 54: 17 says "No weapon that is formed against thee shall prosper; and every tongue that shall rise against thee in judgment

See That You Are A True Inspiration

thou shalt condemn. This is the heritage of the servants of the Lord, and their righteousness is of me, saith the Lord". The thing that devil puts in your way may form, but remember it **WILL NOT** prosper. That is the main reason that God allows his grace and mercy to covers us. The stronger that you become on a spiritual level, the more that the adversary hates it, which causes him to fear us. When soldiers go to war the objective is to overpower the enemy by making them weaker. Once they have created a weak environment, the adversary will start to fear them. This will cause the enemy to back down. That is the same objective in battling with the spiritual warfare's. Be ye not conformed to the world. The world cannot and will not save you.

Finally, my brethren, be strong in the Lord, and in the power of his might. Put on the whole armour of God that ye may stand against the wiles of the devil. For we wrestle not against flesh and blood, but against principalities, against powers, against the rulers of the darkness of this world, against spiritual wickedness in high places.

See That You Are A True Inspiration

Ephesians 6: 10-12

<u>*Day Thirty-Seven Reflections*</u>

Daily Prayer: Ask God to help you to be closer to him in order to have power and sound mind over these things that will try to stop you or pull you astray.

How would you control a spiritual warfare?
_____
_____
_____
_____
_____
_____

Explain the worst thing in which you were tempted with
_____
_____
_____
_____
_____
_____

True Inspiration   *See That You Are A*

Will you ready to fight your through the spiritual warfare's?

_____
_____
_____
_____
_____

<u>*Day Thirty - Eight*</u>

Thought of the day: We all have a gift

Gift: Something given and nothing is expected in return: Something freely given from God: the act of bestowing a favor or item.

Have you ever heard of the saying it is better to give then to receive? We all have a different gift, which allows us to have a different purpose. When

See That You Are A True Inspiration

God gave us Jesus, we were given a gift. Jesus had to die and shed his blood so that we could have a right to the tree of life. God gave us his most precious gift. Some people can be very peculiar when it comes to giving unto others. Most of us will give gifts on special occasions or holiday, because this is something that lies deeply within in our heart. It's called a gift due to us being born to do the things God called us for. It pushes or motivates us each day. A gift from God can consist of a blessing in which we have received. Some may define a gift as a talent. We either knew we had it or never knew that it was inside of us.

Gifts come out once God allows them to show. Some people have different talents, which causes them to have different gifts. A lot of people give gifts only to expect something in return. Get this! You can never live life always expecting things. It doesn't matter if you are on your job, in church, or in a relationship, some things will never be given unto you. The things that we want will begin to come to us in a natural matter. Just as we want them, when we begin to wait on God for these things, he will reveal them to us. I want to encourage everyone to dig a little deeper to really find your gift. Despite the mistakes of the past, everyone still has a gift. We will never find the gift if it is something that isn't being challenged. The key is to work your gift. The gift always starts with us. Talents, gifts, dreams, or visions don't have us. We have them.

A gift must be utilized constantly or it will fade away inside of us. For instance, practice makes perfect. We've all heard of it. Michael Jordan would not have become the person that he is today without some type of gift that caused him to practice for everything. The gift is something of value and it is also something of virtue. Your gift will take you many places if it is utilized in a proper manner. Again, I say some people don't know what their gifts or talents may be. Once you have become closer to God, he will reveal unto you these gifts that you have. As Donald Lawrence says, "the gift it looks good on us". Trust and believe that it is there, because it is in your heart. Do not be complacent in that you don't have a gift. When God created us, he created us with a gift to do work for his kingdom. It's a shame that some people will not want to work for the kingdom. When we work for the kingdom, God has a way to bless us even more. Doing work for the kingdom could be considered as helping around the community. We should remember that during our tenure of life that only what is done for Christ will last. Our gifts to man will soon perish, causing them to never last. Encourage yourself and others, because now is the time for us to operate into the gift that God has given us.

As every man hath received the gift, even so minister the same one to another, as good stewards of the manifold grace of God.

1 Peter 4: 10

See That You Are A True Inspiration

Day Thirty-Eight Reflections

Daily Prayer: Today ask God to reveal to you the things he needs you to do.

What do you feel is your gift?

How would you operate your gift?

What has been stopping you from moving into your gift?

Day Thirty-Nine

Thought of the day: Get closer to God

Close: Not far away or distant: bring together

Have you ever had something that you were always close to? That same very thing, you wanted to love it forever and never let go. You were sad when it was lost. When it was found we were super excited. What if you could become even closer to God? What if we could be closer to God everyday throughout our lifestyle? Get closer to God in your family, relationship, work, school, home, and even church. The key is knowing how to get closer to God. Imagine that the thing we love was gone. We could love God that same very way. Some people have turned on God, but he still found them. One of the ways to become closer to him is being able to devote yourself to him spiritually. We must learn to give God our all. Let the spirit, and heart pour unto him. Let his anointing rule. There has been many times were we have wronged God and never knew it. We should always want to please God with our heart and throughout our actions.

Everything affects God and our spirit. Although, sin may be gratifying for the moment, it always will dismay God. For this reason, it is always important to ask for forgiveness, because you are hurting God as well. The majority of problems that people have are due to them not being close to God or not putting him first in all things. Being close to God means that we must make him first in all things before anything or anyone. The problem that most of us have is lack of faith. Instead of believing in God, we question him. Understand that God always wants us to trust in him, despite the great or the worst. When bills are due, trust in God. Another reason for problems spiritually, or naturally is us not tithing. Tithes are ten percent of our increase. I was in a place where I only tithed occasionally. Do not do it occasionally. Do it every chance that you get. It caused so many problems and headaches due to me not tithing. A financial burden will come over you for your failure to tithe. When we do not tithe we are robbing God. We can never expect to move away from debt if we aren't tithing. Quit allowing the adversary to stop your financial blessing. God wants to increase in our lives; however we must give him the things he deserve.

Those things included are your spirit, heart, love, trust, tithe, time, and your problems. Never give up on God because he will never give up on you. Man cannot ever treat you like God can. Man will never love you the way God can. Man will fail us and leave us; whereas, God said I will never leave you nor forsake you. God would never fail us or even put more on us then we can bare. Allow him to take the burden away and quit trying to take it away for yourself. Now, it is imperative that we allow God to continue to make us over. Yes, we do slip; however grace has kept us. I preached a sermon one Sunday morning entitled "Lord Sit on me" . When my flesh becomes weaken, I need God to sit on me. When I can't take it anymore, I need God to sit on me. Although, I am under attack, I need God to sit on me. For some, God has striped us of some things, because they are not close to him like they should be. Don't go to your grave not knowing who Jesus is. Don't die without trying Jesus for yourself. We all have a choice. That choice is heaven or hell. Whichever one it shall be remember that it is eternity and there is no turning back. I tell people all the time to get their life together while they are still given the chance. I would encourage you to pull yourself closer to God. When all else has failed it was nobody but God.

    Despite the disappointments, it was nobody but God. After the fact that you have become closer to God, he will fix these broken things. When we become closer to God nothing stands in our way. Not even the devil himself could ever stand in our way , because once we have become closer to God the adversary begins to fear us, due to us having power over the adversary and our flesh. Some people will go to church every day; however there is no real relationship with God. Before you can move anywhere with a purpose, you must increase your relationship with God. Get this! God is always greater; therefore that is something that will always put you on the winning team. Having Jesus is the necessity that we cannot live without. I would never know where I would be without Jesus. That's one of the reasons that I am so glad that I know him. In whatever you do, you should always keep God first. That also means you should always want to follow Christ. While you may be in a phase of hurt in your life, it's important to get closer to God. Actually, that is the best time to get closer to God. Always keep God first in everything, so you are able to be blessed.

Submit yourselves therefore to God. Resist the devil, and he will flee from you. Draw nigh to God, and he will draw nigh to you. Cleanse your hands, ye sinners; and purify your hearts, ye double minded.

See That You Are A True Inspiration

James 4:7-8

<u>Day Thirty-Nine Reflections</u>

Daily Prayer: On today say a prayer of repentance and also tell God that you will accept him as your savior.

Have you ever felt astray from God?
_____
_____
_____
_____
_____

How would you want to get closer to God?
_____
_____
_____
_____
_____

True Inspiration   *See That You Are A*

What are some things that you would like to see God do in your life after you have become closer to him?

_____
_____
_____
_____
_____

Day Forty

Thought of the day: Understand yourself

Understand: To know how one reacts to things in life: to know how something works or is supposed to happen: to grasp the reasonableness of behavior: accept the truth: being able to achieve

Have you ever began to wonder about the things that happen in your life? Everything in life happens for a reason. Most of us go days, months, or years without ever understanding ourselves. If you ever looked in a mirror at yourself, would you see something good or bad? Despite the things that you may see, you can fix it. We never understand the decisions we make. We just do make them. It is important that you get a full understanding of your mind, body, spirit and yourself. This helps you to understand your reaction to things. We all have things that we must work on. Some people have been living in denial for so long. They are afraid of the truth about themselves. It an interesting fact that we can be so quick to tell others about themselves, but when the truth is given to us we want to argue or get upset. People don't like to hear the truth about themselves.

Often times we question ourselves or the decisions that we make. What was I thinking about? We ask this question, because at the time we are trying to figure out the things that have happen after they have already happened. My idol Bishop T.D Jakes said, "In all thy learning, get an understanding". Before you begin to jump into a relationship, understand things what your heart needs. There are

See That You Are A True Inspiration

still some things for you for to learn. I hate to say this, but most people do not understand self. Remember that you can be two people. Those two people are your biggest person or your biggest enemy. As you will grow more, you shall understand yourself even more. Here is a tip! Take a sheet of paper and write somethings about yourself that you really love. On the other side write down some areas of improvement. This will help establish a better understanding of you. It doesn't matter that the bad may outweigh the good. Keep this paper and continue to work on your areas of improvement.

It is bad when a person cannot understand himself or herself. Let alone, the decisions that he or she makes. No one other than God will understand you like you can. Your own family, spouse, or best friends cannot understand you. Often time's people think they know us, but in reality they really don't. Get to know yourself. From there, start loving and valuing everything about yourself. It's important to know the things that standout, because they will help you to see yourself. You can't blame anyone for the way that you are. People will even blame God based on the way that they were created. You can't blame the decisions of others for the way that you are. Again, I say it starts with you.

Most people or trying to focus on the outside and they can't see the inside of themselves. Be mindful of the things you say or do. Watch the way that you begin to carry yourself. A person should understand his / her strengths and weakness. A person should also understand his / her character. Part of knowing yourself is knowing the things that make you. These things will drive or motivate you every day. People will have emotional breakdown, because they really don't know themselves. We are strangers to ourselves when we fear to get to know ourselves. We are God's wonderful creation. I would strongly agree that we do need to know others, but it is so important to know yourself first.

See That You Are A True Inspiration

Let us search and try our ways, and turn again to the Lord. Let us lift up our heart with our hands unto God in the heavens.

Lamentations 3: 40-41

<u>Day Forty Reflections</u>

Daily Prayer: Ask God to help you get to know yourself

What is your full name?
_____
_____

Who is this person?
_____
_____
_____
_____
_____
_____

See That You Are A True Inspiration

Why are you the way that you are?

Do you understand yourself (if no then explain why)?

How would you get to know yourself?

Do you know yourself on a spiritual, emotion, physical, or mental level (explain)

True Inspiration   *See That You Are A*

———————————————————————
———————————————————————

What drives you or motivate you?

———————————————————————
———————————————————————
———————————————————————
———————————————————————

What are your likes and dislikes about yourself?

———————————————————————
———————————————————————
———————————————————————
———————————————————————

How would you fix your dislikes?

———————————————————————
———————————————————————
———————————————————————
———————————————————————

How would you love yourself?

———————————————————————
———————————————————————

_____
_____

Why do you love yourself?
_____
_____
_____
_____
_____

Day Forty-One

Thought of the day: The struggle only makes us better

Struggle: To try very hard to do something, or deal with something that may cause problems: moving with difficulty or great effort: something difficult to achieve

As I previously mentioned about experiences, let's incorporate the struggle with experiences. The word "struggle" is known as an opposition of something that we are fighting against. Struggling is something that is good for us because the struggle does make us better. You would not be the person that you are today without some type of struggle. In

See That You Are A True Inspiration

other words, you would not be where you are today without fighting to get there. Some people are struggling on their jobs. Some may even be struggling elsewhere. Every day we struggle with something new. The purpose of a struggle is to improve on growth. For example, a man struggles to lift something, he may be hurting himself for a moment, but his stability to grow is improving.

    The struggle alongside rejection does hurt, but it's only momentary. They say disparities don't last always. Many of people have been struggling for quite some time dealing with things. Sometimes we can try so hard to deal with something, but we realized we don't have the capacity to deal with it. It doesn't matter the size or the way of the struggle. How will you plan to come out? That is the most important part of a struggle. I understand that God will never put more on us then we can bare, but in some things he doesn't want us to struggle in, but we have the tendency to cause harm to ourselves. Some

See That You Are A True Inspiration

people will never want to struggle. You can't just put the cake in the oven. You must go through the entire process. Losing both of my parents, I had struggled with many things. Most people don't know the struggle or difficulties that they are about to face, until they face the challenge. At some point in life we must suffer just for a little awhile. The struggle comes as a test.

God comes that we may have life more abundantly. Don't expect greatness to come without a struggle of getting there. Continue to press into it. Press into things that you desire. The struggles or the past never makes anyone a bad person. God didn't create you to have that mindset that you are a bad person. Every time you struggling God has his hands on you. If you don't believe it, then try him for yourself. Again, we must struggle to get somewhere. God wouldn't allow anyone to struggle if there had not been any good in it. Just as experiences or things that you go through in life will make better, remember that the struggles of life that you endure only make you stronger for who you are. Struggles make us greater in Christ. So I want to encourage you by saying your struggle is over. There will be struggles for as long as you live. It may not be financial or anything else, but it will spiritual. Your struggle is your Goliath and you are David. In other words, it is time to face your giant. We struggle to stay connected with Christ more than anything. Get this! Some people are struggling in their relationships, families, life, or endeavors. Some people may also be struggling in their growth or becoming a better person. It is the fight that we must endure.

Fight the good fight of faith, lay hold on eternal life, whereunto thou art also called, and hast professed a good profession before many witnesses.

1 Timothy 6: 12

Day Forty-One Reflections

Daily Prayer: On today ask God to help you with anything that you may struggle with.

See That You Are A True Inspiration

What are some things you are struggling in?

_____
_____
_____
_____
_____
_____

How do you want to do better for yourself and others that surround you?

_____
_____
_____
_____
_____
_____

Why are you struggling?

_____
_____
_____
_____
_____
_____

Day Forty- Two

Thought of the day: It is time to get down to business

See That You Are A True Inspiration

Business: work that is a part of a job: purposeful activity: an immediate task or objective: movement or action: personal concern.

As you can see from the definitions given unto you from Merriam- Webster's Dictionary, this one word means so many things. Many of us have a lot of different things in which we need to take care of. Now, if you decide to take care of these things then that is up to you. Before God calls us, we must first understand that we have work which is not done. You should wake up each morning wanting to do something different or even change something. It is sad to say, but people in this day in time are not doing what is called of them to do. Some people are just in it for fame, or even worse in it for the money. Money will always be the root to all evil. You have to fully complete something in order to go far.

There are a lot of things that you have to do to help better your community, schools, home, and church. One person cannot do it all. We must learn the ethics of working together. Teachers, Preachers,

Police, Firefighters, EMT's, Doctors, lawyers, etc. we all need you to help this world become a better place. You cannot love what you do if you aren't doing it. A lot of people have quit on the thing(s) that God has ordained them for. This only happens for two reasons. They are either tired or bored with the things they are doing. Some people get drained to where they never wanted to do what God called of them. Even, Isaiah said, "here I am Lord, send me and I will go". It didn't matter if he had to do it by himself, he still done what was expected of him by being obedient. Do it anyhow without complaining. Our emotions will never matter. Things can be done if we allow them to be so. Everything that you do is not always about you. Again, QUIT BEING SELFISH. Allow Jesus to speak to the heart. Don't give in to what the adversary is trying to do. Evil comes due to the body trying influence the soul. That explains the fact that evil will always be present. When we are trying do to good, it seems like there is so much hell that we must go through in order to get there.

It is okay to make a mistake, but do not continue to make the same mistake over and over. Make it your business to do your business. When we get down to business things will begin to change. Do it with love and be obedient. Invest plenty of time in your future. Invest your time in your business. Never forget to invest your time in God. Negative things or even negative people will make every attempt to confuse, misuse, or abuse you in every way they can. For example, notice when we have goals certain people will stop coming around. Some people may just want to be in your business. Remember this one thing! It isn't anyone else's business of where God is taking you. So I am encouraging everyone to get ready to get down to business. Allow the word of God to move throughout your daily life. Sometimes we want God to do everything; however we will not do anything for ourselves. The key is to make something out of nothing. Start something and finish it. In youthful terms, bust a move.

Then said he unto me, fear not, Daniel: for from the first day that thou didst set thine heart to understand, and to chasten thyself before thy God, thy words were heard, and I am come for thy words.

Daniel 10: 12

Day Forty-Two Reflections

Daily Prayer: Ask God to lead and guide you in the direction that he would like to go

What shall your next move be?

_____
_____
_____
_____
_____

What business matter do you have to take care of?

_____
_____
_____

See That You Are A True Inspiration

Are you active in the church, community, with a career, at home, or within an educational program (explain)?

<u>*Day Forty- Three*</u>

Thought of the day: Change your thinking

Thought: an idea, plan, opinion, picture, etc. that is formed in the mind

Our thoughts are something that influence us every day. A person's mind can lead them anywhere. Having a negative mindset can stop you. A negative mindset is something that can set you into a trap or even worse pull you away from God. It is not that serious to allow something to pull you away from

God. Have a positive mindset about things; therefore you will begin to see things being done or accomplished. One bad apple will ruin everything. You can have many positive thoughts, but that one negative thought will mess you up.

The key is to watch your area of focus. In others words, watch what you are thinking. Although, it may be in your mind doesn't mean that you should act on it. After you begin to think about things for so long, you will start to do them. Again, it doesn't matter if your thoughts are good. One negative thought can get you caught up for the remainder of your life. It's sad that when people begin to think negative, they don't realize it. God sees when your mind is not on him. He also sees your negative thoughts. For he knows every one of our thoughts. If you cannot change your mindset, you will continue to have the same outcome.

Another shameful thing is that most people will not change their thoughts even after reading this.

See That You Are A True Inspiration

Some people don't even care to change their way of thinking and living. When you begin to think negative, you are allowing the enemy, and demons into your life to overtake take you. After the thought has occurred, the enemy will use everything he can to get you to do it. For example, people will say they will stop an addiction. After time has passed they have thought about it. Now the adversary brings the temptation and this same person who has struggled to be clean has a choice. Never allow your thoughts to consume you. Nothing will ever be worth going to hell for. For this reason, we should ask for forgiveness if we ever thought negative. Concrete on the good and never the bad. Substitute the negative with all positive thoughts. If you are able to change your thoughts then God will change you.

For I know the thoughts that I think toward you, saith the Lord, thoughts of peace, and not of evil, to give you an expected end.

Jeremiah 29:11

See That You Are A True Inspiration

Day Forty-Three Reflections

Daily Prayer: On today take time to pray that you will not have any bad thoughts by asking God to change your thinking and to also touch you mind.

How will you prevent yourself from getting caught up with your negative thoughts?

_____
_____
_____
_____
_____

What are some positive thoughts in which you have done?

_____
_____
_____
_____
_____

How did negative thinking stop you?

_____
_____

True Inspiration   *See That You Are A*

_____
_____
_____
_____

Explain some negative thoughts that you may have recently had?

_____
_____
_____
_____
_____

<u>Day Forty -Four</u>

Thought of the day: Everything seems good at the beginning

It all seems good at first. Have you ever done something or made a decision? Everything is good, until it blows up in your face. Sometimes we do things that we think will be fair, but it will come back on us. We never expect it to happen. Let alone, we never thought that it would happen to us. Imagine being in relationship like that. The key to any relationship is the two must want to be together. If a person doesn't want to be with you then don't waste your time. Allow them to leave. It's never good to continue to hold on to someone who really doesn't care about you. People that love or even care so much are the first to get hurt. Many of us have fought ourselves in relationships. We have went from relationship to relationship thinking that we were with "the one". You should never assume that you are with that person for whom is for you. First, you must make sure this person is the one that God has sent to you. Another key point to any relationship is love. That is right I said the "L Word". Love gives people a different viewpoint. It gives a person the ability to think and look on the positive side. Love always outweighs the bad in relationships.

    We don't understand the ways of keeping something great to make it last. People will no longer continue to deal with the foolishness of others after a certain period. The truth is, no one wants to be with someone who doesn't know how to carry him/herself. People will no longer put up with others mistreating them, not making them happy, or disrespecting them through actions or words. Actions will always speak louder than words. Humans can take so much. Why would anyone want to be somewhere that he / she is not happy? Look at it this way, every Queen wants her King, while every King needs his Queen. Things like a bad relationship will teach us many things. My wife to soon to be will get all of my love, time, etc.

You would not want to be with anyone who really doesn't love you. A relationship can never stand without some type of foundation being set. God must be in the relationship because he is the head. One thing that can cause relationships to fail is expecting too much. Although, our expectations can be over the top, we should not pressure anyone. Sometimes it could be best keeping these things to yourself and allow the person to do what he / she can. This is the one factor that will mess us up every time. Things that happen inside a relationship should be kept confidential between the two, unless it is a critical emergency. It doesn't matter who it may be. They should not be in your relationship and you should not give them room to be there.

Before jumping into something make sure he / she is that one person that you would want to spend the rest of your life with. Love is not boasting or bragging. Sometimes we will need space. No one wants to come home from a stressful day to get ready to argue. Love is persistent. It will not argue constantly. People are so quick to ask God to send them a great person, then when it happens they want something that was never in his will. That is something that has always confused me. So remember it takes two. The biggest thing is to always put God first next to the significant other. Having said that, extend the relationship with God.

See That You Are A True Inspiration

Let thy tender mercies come unto me, that I may live: for thy law is my delight.

Psalms 119:17

Day Forty-Four Reflections

Daily Prayer: If you are in a relationship ask God to continue to bless your relationship so that the two of you can grow together?

>** Please continue to answer the questions even if you aren't in a relationship**

What are things that you have experienced in your relationship?

_____
_____
_____
_____
_____
_____

See That You Are A True Inspiration

How have these things changed your relationship?
_____
_____
_____
_____
_____

Explain the things that you would like to see happen in your relationship?
_____
_____
_____
_____
_____

How do you plan on growing together?
_____
_____

Day Forty Five

Thought of the day: Communication is the best tool

Communication: the act of using words, sounds, signs, or behavior to express or exchange information or thoughts to share; make known.

Communication is always important. It is a factor of everything that we do in life. Without communication you can never have anything, nor will you get in anywhere. Police officers are a prime example. They are always communicating with the command center. They would not get anywhere without the aid of the command center directing them. When we are communicating with God, we will allow him to steer us into the place that we should be. Communication plays a key role in all things. We should always communicate. We communicate with our job, church, and our families. This is a way to let them know the events that have occurred. A trait for this is called expressing ourselves. You should be able to speak the truth without others becoming offended. You should be able to speak with others without someone becoming angry. Everything in life revolves around some type of language being used.

Continue to be mindful of the words that you use. This tool is used in order to maintain some type of understanding. Communication is something that will speak for itself. It's the language used to translate our emotions for one another. It could also be used to translate love. We as people should always communicate with God about everything we do. While speaking to God, the devil will try his best to either interpretate or intercept the information spoken to God. Once again the adversary doesn't want us to receive blessings and favor from God.

Communication with each other is always our best tactic. You are able to use this skill by opening your heart. People that don't communicate are afraid of some things or they chose not to open their heart just yet. You cannot make others speak to you. It will come when they are ready. This is a strong technique used to build relationships every single day. Women

See That You Are A True Inspiration

dread when men cannot talk to them in a relationship. Some people have been taught to keep things inside. Allowing our communication skills to develop more, we find ourselves getting closer to our love ones. The most important factor again to get closer to God. Communication is one of the best ways that will help grow a strong bond.

Then the Lord put forth his hand, and touched my mouth. And the Lord said unto me, Behold, I have put my words in thy mouth.

Jeremiah 1:9

Day Forty-Five Reflections

Daily Prayer: Allow God to help you to communicate better by asking him to give you the necessities of words to say among others.

In your own words explain communication or what it may mean to communicate?

_____
_____
_____

See That You Are A True Inspiration

Why should we communicate with others?

Have you ever been in a place where you did not want to communicate?

What is most important about communication?

Day Forty - Six

Thought of the day: Stop complaining

Complaining: expression of grief or pain; something which causes outcry or protest; something one may not like.

Why is it that people complain? People will complain when they are in pain or something has become distasteful. A lot of us are guilty of doing this. Some may do it more than others. Complaining is a cry for help. Complaining is also used as a method to seek attention from others. Complaining never gets us anywhere. In fact it leaves you confused or frustrated. Instead of always complaining, you should do things that are expected of you. People who complain will never get their way. Everyday people struggle to complain about something.

For example, men are taught to always be tough and never complain. My mother is a prime example of a woman who never thought to complain. Despite, ALS taking over her body I never heard her complain the about the pain that she had going through. My mother who would always say, "Thank you Jesus." Instead of complaining the key is to always say tell God thank you. My mother was a beautiful rose. She always had a smile on her face. How can someone go through so much and still have a smile on their face? We can smile knowing that we are hold onto God. When we acknowledged God with the fruit of our lips, he will ease the pain away. Always thank God anyhow for your good and bad days.

Some of you may have felt like giving up. It was never intended for you to give up on something that God has given you. I never knew what she was going through in her body, but her fight gave me strength every day. It encouraged me more. It is sad that people will find the littlest things to complain over. People will take things that are so small and turn them into something bigger then they seem. At some point people should get tired of waking up every day to complain. Life is not intended to complain.

Some things that you go through in life are actually intended to make you stronger, but people would never think about it like that. People will complain due to them not seeing a way through something. Every day we complain about something. Again, we will not even know that we are doing such thing. God has brought us way too far to be complaining. Having said that, you should not complain, but accept it. After being able to accept something, it will give you the ability to move on from things that have hurt you. You are hurting yourself by complaining. Complaining can cause stress, depression, headaches, wearisome, and fear. It can also cause us to miss out on God. That is too much to have, so I will pass on complaining. Again,

See That You Are A True Inspiration

give your problems to God. Learn by it and live your life without complaining.

Do all things without murmurings and disputings

Philippians 2:14

<u>*Day Forty-Six Reflections*</u>

Daily Prayer: On today ask God to help you get through this day without doing anything of complaining.

What are the main reasons people complain?
_____
_____
_____
_____
_____

How would you change your thinking and the way others think about complaining?
_____
_____
_____

See That You Are A
True Inspiration

_____
_____

What attitude do you have in order to help you cease complaining?

_____
_____
_____
_____
_____

In your own words explain what Philippians 2: 14 - 15 means to you?

_____
_____
_____
_____
_____

Use this section to write a vow to God, yourself, and any others of how you plan not to ever complain from this day on

_____
_____
_____
_____
_____

See That You Are A True Inspiration

Day Forty-Seven

Thought of the day: The addiction will kill you

Addiction: A compulsion or habit: strong and harmful need to regularly have something or do something: something that is hard to get away from.

An addiction is usually something that is not easy to get away from. An addiction is caused by one that can't live without something. There are many addicts in this world. No one is ever born with an addiction. They have been introduced to the addiction. Now, it has taken its toll over that person's life and his or her family. An addiction is something that has caused the person to draw from God. Any type of addiction is never good. As people will begin to tap into these additions more, they are allowing it to constantly grow by continuously feeding that addiction.

See That You Are A True Inspiration

People will never tell you that they are addicts of something; however most people can tell by a person's spirit or humility. Living with an addict is just as worse as being one. They will pressure others into doing something. For some addicts they are attached to the things they do. Being an addict can cause more problems in life than anything. Most of the time an addict does not think until afterwards. An addict is so horrible that they will kill for the thing in which they are seeking, just as anything in the wild will prey upon a catch. Addicts go through all kinds of hell to get what they want. An addict doesn't realize that they are killing themselves spiritually, emotionally, mentally, and physically. The addict has allowed the flesh to overpower them. For this cause the addict is dying spiritually.

This thing that they are attached to have consumed them. An addict can be anyone involved in drugs, alcohol, trafficking, pornography, gambling, or adultery. Of course, all these addictions are sins that God condemns. It behooves me to hear to that addicts rather chose the addiction over their own family. It is sad that addicts will do their dirt in front of their own children. I never knew that an addiction could ever be that serious. It is bad enough that our youth are expose to more now than ever before. This is a spiritually demon connected to them to pull them away from God, church, and family. Most addicts do the addiction for fun, after -which they will feel guilty that they have done it. They also feel like they have shamed God, which in fact they have. God is not pleased with these types of actions going against his kingdom. Now, I must say this, anyone can change; however once the change has occurred stay away from anything that may cause temptations. God can deliver anyone if they would like to be delivered. Don't allow the spirit to die. Feed your spirit by becoming closer to God in order to fight the good fight. At some point it will become old and no longer of use.

See That You Are A True Inspiration

There hath no temptation taken you but such as is common to man: but God is faithful, who will not suffer you to be tempted above that ye are able; but will with the temptation also make a way to escape, that ye may be able to bear it.

1 Corinthians 10:13

Day Forty-Seven Reflections

Daily Prayer: Say a prayer that God will cover you so that you are tempted into any addiction. Also pray over someone's life who may have an addiction.

Have you ever been tempted with an addiction (explain)?

_____
_____
_____
_____
_____
_____

If you ever had an addiction explain it

_____
_____

See That You Are A True Inspiration

How did you recover?

How would you plan to be a blessing to someone who has an addiction?

Day Forty-Eight

Thought of the day: There is a reason for your season

Season: Changing of something: Making different: Making new.

See That You Are A True Inspiration

We are coming a point in life where seasons are changing. For example, I look at how the weather changes, causing different types of temperatures. The leaves begin to change colors and they begin to fall. Let's look at like this. We are the tree that God has rooted to never die. Those leaves that fall would be life. As a tree that stands; although its leaves are gone its job is to stand strong. Despite the treacherous conditions that you have been put through, your job is always stand strong. People tried to cut your strength; although your stability fell for quite some time, you begun to trust in God which made us grow again. The point is that we all go through seasons. They can be good seasons or even horrible seasons. As long as you are rooted deeply in God, then you will never go anywhere else. Be like that tree and never move. We can never allow the season to change us.

Some people are going places. The problem that most of us have is the fact that we never understand our season. People want the best, so they must be the best. Seasons come with the ability to change a person. There is a season for everything. God wanted you to prosper; therefore it is your season. Things may not go your way, due to God letting you know that it is not your season; however it will come. There is a reason for your season. Some people come into your life for a reason, while others want to be seasonal ones. Seasonal people are people who come and go in our life. Understand this one important factor, the season could be used for a test of faith, but I guarantee you that it will take you higher. I would encourage others that it is there season of overflow.

God will send blessings that will run over; however we must wait. Steve Harvey said, "God may not allow things to happen right now, due to us needing more growth in some areas, or even more humility". God wouldn't allow anything to happen or come your way that will destroy you; therefore his primary job is to cover you from evil people or evil things. God has placed people in your life to help cover you. Some people or things God had removed out of our life, because they never meant us any good.

For many us, God is taking us higher. The key for a season is grace and favor. Sometimes I just think of the grace and favor that God has restored upon my life. Don't try to change the season. If we must decide to change, it must for a reason. You should understand where God is taking you. It's time to walk into your season. Ye, thou I walk through the shadow of death, I must still move into my season. It's your time. It's your season. You don't see it now, but it is your season. Everything is not going well, but it is your season. I understand that things are tight and your back may be up against the wall. I heard God say purpose, overflow, and success will be coming your way. Do the things that God ordained for you.

For he shall be as a tree planted by the waters, and that spreadeth out her roots by the river, and shall

See That You Are A True Inspiration

not see when heat cometh, but her leaf shall be green; and shall not be careful in the year of drought, neither shall cease from yielding fruit.
Psalms 1:3

Day Forty-Eight Reflections

Daily Prayer: On today ask God to give you the ability to walk into your season.

Do you feel that it is your season for things to work in your favor?

_____
_____
_____
_____
_____

Where do you want God to take you?

_____
_____
_____
_____
_____

See That You Are A
True Inspiration

In your own words explain Psalms 1:3

_____
_____
_____
_____
_____
_____

Day Forty- Nine

Thought of the day: Living in anger

Anger: A strong feeling of being upset due to something going wrong or bad: the feeling that makes others want to sin:

Being angry causes many feelings or belief. This word means a lot. The main feeling that causes anger is displeasure or when things are not going our way. "Anger is a bold emotion of frustration felt and displayed by God and man", according to Nelsons Student Bible Dictionary. How can we make God angry? We make God angry or displeased in things we do that he is not pleased with. These things include, lying, lust, abomination, failure to put him first, etc. Just to name a few. Sin is the one thing that displeases God. I never understood the reason that people become angry so quick or the reason that people wake up angry.

A lot of things that we go through can cause us to get bitter in our spirit. Some things will cause us to become angry with God. This was something I was dealing with after losing my father. I knew the reason that I became angry; although for some people they will never realize why they are angry. I had got into a phase where I became un-pleased with how things were going. I had just lost my mother six months ago. Now I must deal with this. It was to the point where I became upset with God. From there, it will cause us to become ill. A person angered in his or her soul will do things unexpected or things that shouldn't be done. It is okay to feel upset or frustrated; however we should never allow our frustration to turn into something that it should not be. Being frustrated or upset is human nature. You should never allow it to become the best of you.

Some people do different things when they are angry to help them cool down. This helps us get our mind back together. It's important that you never allow people steal your joy by making you angry. They want to steal your joy because that it what the adversary does. Think about that for a second. It could be something so little turned into something so big. As previously stated, while we are angry we need self -control. Self-control gives us the ability to look at situations different without the temptation involved. We call it self-control, which helps us control self. Often times when we are angry or upset our flesh becomes our weakness. While these emotions are running wild, our flesh or the enemy tells us to take revenge, commit the crime, fall into temptation, fall for lust, commit adultery or even worse stop believing in God because he never there. People are behind bars or even dead due to them being so angry that they allowed the factors above to become the main their main factor. Sometimes we mess up our lives or lives of others with angriness. This is known as expressing ourselves, which in fact is good for us to let it out the right way. Never provoke others while they are angry. In fact this may be the reason that others become angry. They have been either provoked in a relationship, school, work, or in their families. The best way to deal with angriness is by talking to God. He is the one that has the key to our hearts.

Be ye angry, and sin not: let not the sun go down upon your wrath: neither give place to the devil.

Ephesians 4:26-27

True Inspiration

<u>*Day Forty-Nine Reflections*</u>

Daily Prayer: Ask God to help you control your anger

What are some things that have made you angry?

_____
_____
_____
_____
_____

What are some ways that you get over your angriness?

_____
_____
_____
_____
_____

How did you feel after you released your anger?

_____
_____
_____
_____
_____

True Inspiration

Have you ever been angry with God (explain)?

_____
_____
_____
_____
_____

How would you control you angriness?

_____
_____
_____
_____
_____

Day Fifty

Thought of the day: Be careful of the ones lending you a hand

Help: causing something to be less severe: benefit from something

Have you ever been on the side of the road stranded or needing someone to help you? You would never be able to move until someone comes to the rescue. Imagine that being the same way when

See That You Are A True Inspiration

you are in dire need of help, but it never came. How would that feel in need of help, but it is nowhere to be found? God wanted me to encourage you that help is on the way. It may not be seen now, but it is coming. Remember in all things that you do it is found in God. It is always important to help others. By all means we all need help. Helping someone is the one thing that is beneficial to others. I understand that most people love the fact of being independent. We don't want others to help us. The fact of receiving help from others scares us. We are afraid of what others think of us or the things they will say about us.

    A smile or the way one dresses doesn't mean that one has it all together. While we are in need of help some people will not help. It doesn't matter where we are or the way it has happened. It is beneficial to others that they love to see our struggle. Believe it or not it is very true. Something it is interesting at the fact that they will laugh at us and begin to share our information with others. Know your circle and your limitations. A lending hand could also give advice. Everyone isn't for you; however some people are not against you. Actually, some people want to help you. Some people who are in your life want to see you succeed and they will do everything that they can to help you in any way possible.

The main question is why do people say if you ever need anything then I'm here? They are saying that because they are trying to be sympathetic. You know that they won't be there. They will just be in your way or in your business. Some people are there but not there. Allow me to explain. Some people are in your life, but don't want to give you their time. I have always helped people or attempted to get help for people. The world doesn't owe you anything. Never allow things to lead you astray. Always know who to ask and who not to ask.

Be cautious of the things that you allow. That means be cautious of who you allow to have your

See That You Are A True Inspiration

weakness. Ask yourself will these people help make me to be strong? Some people are dying to use everything against you. Please understand that. The objective is to be wise in all things. We know of the ones that want to help, because God has strictly given them unto us for this main reason. You should never want the ones that you love to feel helpless or hopeless. Remember there are people helping you every day. Some may do it different. Again, be cautious of people who you allow in your business or to help you. God says your good works will not go in vein.

Ask, and it shall be given you; seek, and ye shall find; knock, and it shall be opened unto you.

Matthew 7:7

<u>*Day Fifty Reflections*</u>

See That You Are A True Inspiration

Daily Prayer: Ask God to help you to become wiser in things you ask people for, so that it won't hurt you.

What are some things that you have needed assistance on?

_____
_____
_____
_____
_____

How do you feel being stranded (meaning struggling but no one is there)?

_____
_____
_____
_____
_____

What are some ways that you will better help people?

_____
_____
_____
_____
_____

True Inspiration   *See That You Are A*

Day Fifty - One

Thought of the day: love me for me

As previously stated, we know what love means. Let's incorporate love me for me with love has so much power. We know that there is power in love. What exactly does it mean to say "love me for me"? I understand that we should love people as for who they are. Some things cannot be loved. Some people will use the excuse that "God loves me for who I am, so why can't you "? Have you ever noticed that sometimes we put too much empathizes on God? In fact God does loves us, but he does not love the sinful acts that we do. That is something to think about. Many people want us to accept them for their flaws and everything that they have to offer. You can love someone, but you will never love the flaws of a person. The flaws are the past; therefore we should never love the past. We should be focused on the future.

We want others to approve of things that we should not do in general. How would it possible to allow others to love us if we are not committed? Better yet, how would it be possible to allow others to love us if we are still making the same mistakes? Many people are put in situations where they are forced to love someone. For an example, you should never be forced to love someone, or their bad habits that they still have. Love is not forceful. Most people will use the excuse that God knows their heart or they want someone to pray that they get delivered. The problem is people don't want to be delivered.

You can have someone's heart, but it is impossible to love someone's habits. I recently had a discussion on this topic. People will love others for who they are and not what they've done. That means there is something deeper than what you have done.

See That You Are A True Inspiration

It is looking beyond the habits. For example, Jesus will look at the heart. Some people cannot take the habits of another person, nor will they put up it. We must ask ourselves in these type of situations whether or not it is worth our love and our time. If in fact it is not then we should no longer continue to put up with certain things. Sometimes we allow lust to get in the way of what God is saying. Some people feel like they can love someone's bad habits. People with bad habits should allow themselves time to get themselves together before jumping into a relationship.

Love is patient, love is kind. It does not envy, it does not boast, it is not proud. It does not dishonor others, it is not self-seeking, it is not easily angered, and it keeps no record of wrongs. Love does not delight in evil but rejoices with the truth. It always protects, always trusts, always hopes, always perseveres. Love never fails. But where there are prophecies, they will cease; where there are tongues, they be stilled; where there is knowledge, it will pass away.

1 Corinthians 13: 4-8

True Inspiration See That You Are A

Day Fifty-One Reflections

Daily Prayer: Ask God on today to help you with the ability to love someone for who they are and not what they have done.

Have you ever been forced to loved or felt that way?

_____
_____
_____
_____
_____

What would help you to better love someone?

_____
_____
_____
_____
_____

Explain 1 Corinthians 13: 4-8 in your own words

_____
_____
_____
_____
_____

See That You Are A True Inspiration

Use this section to write things about love_____
_____
_____
_____
_____
_____
_____
_____

Day Fifty- Two

Thought of the day: You are worth more than that

Worth: An amount of something valued

What are you worth? Have you ever took much needed time to detail a vehicle, or a house? People will take care of the things that they have been blessed with. Sometimes it gets junky, but we keep these things clean. Compare this to your life. Sometimes you mess up and God still cleanses you. The objective is to take care of yourself. Despite the fact that you may have had a horrible childhood, or that you may have some skeletons in your closet, you are worth something. You are valued more than just a dollar. There are people in today's society who will never have any self-worth. Steve Harvey said, " In order to be a success, you have to act like a success". Well, I am saying "that you must also walk like a success". I had never had a million dollars, but I will always walk and talk like I do.

When people don't have any worth, they are not valuing themselves. No self-worth causes feelings of doubt, betrayal, no self-esteem, depression, stress, or even worse thoughts of suicide. Some people will say that they were never given any self-worth, because they have always been misunderstood, looked at the wrong way, or judged for something they are not. Society has way of labeling people. Everywhere that we go we are given a label. This label is used to identify people without their full name being used. For example, our background history can be pulled up with our name, which then identifies us as who we are. If you see a duck then it is a duck. You are what you are. Another example would be a woman dressing immodest to get attention and she gets called something inappropriate or men wearing their pants below their knees. I used those examples only to help portray some things. You should value yourself. Invest more time in yourself. We all are worth One million dollars, but we rob the value of ourselves more than depositing great things into our lives, or our future.

Great things will always start with us. We rob ourselves by not thinking positive or finding ways that will help us motivate ourselves. Despite the lies that people have told or the way that you have been treated, I want you to understand that God has ability to be more than your haters. God has given you the ability to be more than who they think you are. God will give them the ability to see you for who you are. He will allow them to see where your heart lies. It doesn't matter what they said, you are always worth more than that. People will not give anyone a bad label if they carry themselves up to par. Your worth is your lifestyle. Sometimes we go through so much that eating healthy is a played out factor. A lot of toxins has been deposited into the body; whereas some people do not care of what they have placed into the body. A lot of things begin to get better and easier for us when you understand your true worth.

    You matter, because you are valued. Despite, at one point that you were never able to see these things, know that God will always care. People never really talk about us, we talk about ourselves because we are allowing it or we are answering to it. That is something to think about. When thinking of this, we should never compare ourselves to others or envy those around us. Again, the key is to value what God has created. That means accept you for what you are worth. Despite, things that people attempt to place in your head. Value your appearance. If you cannot value yourself or your appearance then you will get

See That You Are A True Inspiration

treated the way you dress. We take pride in many things other than ourselves. Quit allowing things and people to get the best of you by telling you that you aren't worth anything. God created you to be more than you may think that you are worth.

For whatsoever is a man profited, if he shall gain the whole world, and lose his own soul? Or what shall a man give in exchange for his soul?

Matthew 16: 26

Day Fifty-Two Reflections

Daily Prayer: Ask God to give you more understanding of your worth to help boost your self-esteem.

On a scale from one-ten what would you rate yourself and why?

_____
_____
_____
_____
_____

See That You Are A True Inspiration

What are some things that you mostly value about yourself?

_____
_____
_____
_____
_____

What are some things that you would least value about yourself and why?

_____
_____
_____
_____
_____

How would you begin to value yourself?

_____
_____
_____
_____
_____

In order to value yourself, there must be self-worth. How would you find your self-worth without the help of people?

See That You Are A
True Inspiration

What are you worth?

Day Fifty - Three

Thought of the day: It's by the grace of God

Grace: unmerited favor; mercy; compassion; kindness

Have you ever been in a situation that you needed grace? We all need grace. Grace is compared to forgiveness. When you have forgave others or vice versa, you are showing them grace. Imagine what life would be like without grace. Grace comes to never go anywhere. So many of us have really let God down; however he cares for us. That means in spite of our mistakes God has showed us favor to continue to move on. It is hard being a Christian. The key word in Christian is "Christ". For Christians the objective is to be like Christ. I understand we are not perfect; however we care less about our mistakes.

Grace is something that God shows you constantly. Exodus 34:6 says that God is merciful and gracious, long suffering, and abundant in goodness and truth. In spite of us not deserving grace, God still shows it. That is really something to think about. Grace is what has kept us through our life. Grace is something that is always being taken for granted, yet it still comes. Please don't get holier than thou in this section. I hear many people claim reasons that they never needed grace. Never think for a second that you could have done anything without grace. The problem is not enough people are real. People will not care to tell their mistakes, because they are ashamed. Sometimes I think of the times I should have been dead or even worse locked up behind bars; although grace and mercy kept me. Again, I say do not get holier than thou when reading this.

As a minister I will find that too many people mess up by doing the same thing, only to around to continue to ask for forgiveness. God is a God of many promises that he will always keep. Unfortunately, the sad thing is people will constantly make promises to God and never keep them. Some of you have the give and take attitude with God. That means God I will stop doing that if you bless me with that. This will mess you up every time. God knows if or not you are speaking from the heart. It was grace that made you who or what you are today. An interesting fact is that it only took five quarts of Jesus blood to cover us in our sins. That means to make us who we are he had to

See That You Are A True Inspiration

shed his blood for us. God has to wipe away our sins in order for us to be who he wants us to be. Some people believe that grace will never run out; however the moment that is your last, grace has then ran out. Nothing about you is so wrong that God cannot fix you. Some people thought they have failed. I am here to encourage you that you are not a failure. God stills loves you. Nothing shall be able to change you by the grace of God. Encourage yourself by saying "IT'S BY THE GRACE OF GOD". You are still here because of the grace of God. Through the grace we shall overcome and get through. I'm so glad that God has showed me favor.

And he said unto me, my grace is sufficient for thee: for my strength is made perfect in weakness. Most gladly therefore will I rather glory in my infirmities, that the power of Christ may rest upon me.

2 Corinthians 12: 9

<u>Day Fifty-Three Reflections</u>

Daily Prayer: Ask God to continue to give you grace for things

In your own words explain grace
_____
_____
_____
_____
_____

Why does God give us grace?
_____
_____
_____
_____
_____

Why do you deserve grace?
_____
_____
_____
_____
_____

Day Fifty - Four

See That You Are A True Inspiration

Thought of the day: It is time to step it up

Step- moving into a greater location

Before you can walk, you must first crawl? As babies get older they learn to crawl first. Some of us are still crawling with many things, because we cannot learn how to walk. We have many things that we need to step up on; whereas we are doing a lot of nothing. The community we live in would become BETTER if everyone done their part. If we joined together as one we could make a change. We live in a world where we don't have a voice anymore. People have ignored the truth to start living a lie. The blind is leading the blind. The work must first be done. The key is taking things one step at a time. Some people will never know right from wrong. Two people who are wrong will never be focused on doing right. We have a lot to do. I admire those who are working diligently to be something in order to turn the communities into everything. People are no longer taking initiative because of them being so comfortable with the way things are that they will care less to change it. Change starts with you. I commend those fathers who are in their child's life. Men we need you because you are who God has chosen to do a wonderful mission. Ladies and gentlemen your goal is to help build this world. Nothing can be done without you. There are many ways to go about making change. A lot of people are doing enough just to get by, when we need to be giving our all.

Have not I commanded thee? Be strong and of good courage; be ye not afraid, neither be thou dismayed: for the Lord thy God is with thee whithersoever thou goest.

Joshua 1:9

Day Fifty-Four Reflections

See That You Are A True Inspiration

Daily Prayer: Ask God to increase in you and move you out the way to decrease

How shall you step things up?
_____
_____
_____

What things shall you do in the community?
_____
_____
_____
_____
_____

What things do you want to make better?_____
_____
_____
_____
_____
_____

How will you make a difference in your community?
_____
_____
_____

See That You Are A True Inspiration

<u>*Day Fifty- Five*</u>

Thought of the day: Being in an almost situation

Almost: Only little less than

Every day we go through life in an almost situation. We are there, but we are not quite there. An almost situation is something that can be controlled before it escalates. Most of the time the situations we face are just test. Life involves test every day. It is up to you whether you pass or fail. The best thing to always do is to lean on God; although your faith, and patience are being tested. People and certain things will love to place us in an almost situation. We could find ourselves on the job being placed in an almost situation. Again these things happen to us every day. The objective is to be quick thinking. An example would be feeling or acting on something that would not be right. These situations come after we have had more than enough. Before too long it could get out of hand if it is not controlled. The challenge, opportunity, or desire will always present itself. This cannot steal the joy of God's people. It only will do that if we allow to. No matter what we may do, as a Christian there will be many almost situations.

People will push you to the limit and love to put you in an almost situation. People can only take so much. Some people were almost in the perfect

See That You Are A True Inspiration

destination; however some people have let go too quick. Even when we are being tested, we must learn the appropriate way to handle it. The key is patience. Luckily, God will always shield us. Almost situations are life. An almost situation can either make or break someone. These are the things that will come unexpected and they will almost happen. Sometimes the adversary will have ways of testing our patience or our faith. It seems like it will always be something after what we have just dealt with. Learn the situation. From there, learn to conquest over it. When we have faith it gives us the ability to understand that God has everything planned out. Before you get to the breaking point you are at the almost point. That is when you need to be praying. The situation that was almost could be flipped into a purposeful situation. Almost situations can intend on helping you or mislead you into the wrong things.

I know both how to be abased, and I know how to be abound; everywhere and in all things I am instructed

See That You Are A True Inspiration

both to be full and to be hungry, both to abound and to suffer need.

Philippians 4: 12

Day Fifty-Five Reflections

Daily Prayer: Ask God to bring you out of that situation by simply being with you today so he will cover and protect you from any situation.

How would you explain an almost situation that occurred in your life?

_____
_____
_____
_____
_____

Are you being set free?

_____
_____
_____
_____
_____

See That You Are A True Inspiration

What ways would you control the situation before it escalates?
_____
_____
_____
_____
_____

How would you handle yourself in an almost situation?
_____
_____
_____
_____
_____

<u>Day fifty- Six</u>

Thought of the day: Make everything in life count

When you make things count, you are going the extra mile to finish something once created. You should learn to accept things for what they are as you grow and learn. Everything done in life should count toward something. Every word that is proclaimed should mean something. That means it is so important that we make everything count. Life is too short not to do something that would count toward something or even attempt to help others. It is always worth the try. Nothing would ever count if we are regretful or doubtful amongest ourselves. Some people have made it up in their mind that they no longer count, or they are no longer are worthy of anything. Some may even feel as if God has counted them out; however God will never count us out.

People exclude themselves away from many things, because the lack of help or knowledge. With the help of Christ we cannot exclude ourselves or even feel excluded. Things will begin to count once we believe. The objective is to start with nothing and watch it turn into something. As God created the world, he had to start with something. How would God create the world in seven days? He took dirt to make man. Another key part is standing still. A lot of people do not know when to stand still. If you fall for anything then you will stand for nothing. You are failing when you cannot make things count. Learn to be effective not defective. Another key aspect is to impact the lives of others. Make a difference some type of way. Be productive in all things. You must learn to be effective at home, on the job, in college, in relationships, in church, and in your life. It is a waste of time, and energy to not be effective.

Wake up to do the extraordinary in order to be extraordinary. Do something that you never thought could or would be done. Some people love to standout, which is okay; however you should allow God to reveal you. It's not about being bigger than the next person or even having the big head. Never get to grown or big that you fail to own up to your mistakes, because God will shut you down before you even think that you are too big to do his will. Change starts with what we will do today. The things you make count should always count to you. Always count your blessings. Always learn to accept

See That You Are A True Inspiration

things and people for what they are. Make every second count and be thankful of those many things. It always feels good on the inside to make a difference somewhere. So today is the day to make it count. Ready. Set. Go

Redeeming the time, because the days are evil.

Ephesians 5: 16

Day Fifty-Six Reflections

Daily Prayer: Ask God to help you make everything that he has placed in your life count.

What are some things you want to make count?

_____
_____
_____
_____
_____

How will you do these things before it is too late?

_____
_____

See That You Are A True Inspiration

In what ways are you effective?

How do you feel that you may be ineffective?

True Inspiration   *See That You Are A*

Day Fifty- Seven

Thought of the day: Live your life, but not your social media life.

When people ask you to allow them to live their life, you should do just that. In order to live life some people must find out the hard way. Sometimes I wish that I could still go to my parents for advice on different things. Life is Life. The things that you allow to form are a way of life. There are many things that you must understand. The things in life that you do cannot change. We meet many people and cannot treat them fair. I've even heard people quoting "you only live once". In fact that is very true. We never get a second at life, but that doesn't mean to take yours by doing something outrageous or something that will cost you for the remainder of your life. Some people will explain the only things they've done in life. Those things include eat, sleep, party, work, and social media.

People will claim that they have no life. Allow me to elaborate for a second. There are 24 hours in a day. How much time do we spend on social media? A lot of people can spend their entire day using social media. We spend more time posting / posing for the media and will never give our families, job, God, or relationships any time. Social media is a huge problem that we are facing in today's time. One of the attributes of life is social media. It is everywhere. It is all over the world. Mostly everyone has some type of social media. Social media is something that has gotten far out of hand. We cannot change it, because it is something that has over-ruled us in many ways. Social media has overtaken the state of mind or the state of well-being of people. Social media has the tendency to destroy many things. By all means there can be some things on social media that are very interesting. Some people have used it as a tool to reconnect to others. Some have even used it to destroy others. People will even be in Church using social media. It's sad that we will miss out on a perfect opportunity of becoming closer to Christ.

A person's social media life isn't important. Social Media is another extracurricular activity. People will deactivate / delete a social media page and still worry about what is going on. Just as the adversary attempts to destroy or pull us away from Christ, he will use social media as an even bigger temptation. You should always be aware and be careful of the things that you are posting. It can be used to find someone or even used as a tactic to be in a person's business. One thing that you must understand is that you should not post it if would offend anyone. If you would not do or say it around your loved ones, then it should not be thought about.

See That You Are A True Inspiration

There is no reason to post inappropriate behavior or language onto the social media sites. People are always watching and waiting to destroy someone. By all means, I do not say not to have social media, but you should be cautious of things you place on social media. The wrong thing placed on social sites can destroy a person for quite some time. This could also be known as cyber - bullying.

But sanctify the Lord God in your hearts: and always be ready always to give an answer to every man that asketh you a reason of the hope that is in you with meekness and fear.

1 Peter 3:15

Day Fifty-Seven Reflection

Daily Prayer: Ask God to forgive of inappropriate things placed on social media. Also ask him to guide you when posting, so that you are a light to others.

What is the purpose of social media?
_____
_____
_____
_____

True Inspiration   *See That You Are A*

_____

_____

How do you use your social media?

_____

_____

_____

_____

_____

Has it ever destroyed you?

_____

_____

_____

_____

_____

Will you change the way that you utilize social media?

_____

_____

_____

Have you ever been a light to others using social media?

_____

_____

See That You Are A True Inspiration

_____
_____
_____

How much time do you spend using social media?_____

_____
_____
_____
_____

Day Fifty- Eight

Thought of the day: It's in your account

Account: something we make a deposit in; actions of a person

Most people have an account where they make deposit or withdraws. Imagine if there was an account for all of our actions. I'm sure with all the mistakes I've made, it would make me rich. I never understood the reason that people aren't accountable for their own actions. They want to blame others for something, which is never good. There is an account of which everything that you do, which means a record is being kept. God keeps an account of everything we do in life. Everything is being deposited into this account. When you die then you will have to give God an explanation of everything that you have done in life. Start depositing good things into your account. Often time's people try to hide or run away from God. In fact, you cannot hide your sins, nor can you hide from God. God has eyes everywhere in your life. It starts with the heart. Things that are deposited in the heart could be a good lifestyle or even a bad lifestyle.

Everything that we do matters, because everything has a spirit attached to it. That spirit could be a not so good one. From there it has become a part of your daily life. Now it is has become something that you must fight through every day. People want to go to heaven, but the sad thing is everyone will not make it there. This world has become so detritus or blind to many things. The world has taken its focus off of God; however God is still the truth. Despite what the world thinks holiness, purity, cleanness, etc. is still right. People will minister to others through dancing, singing, or preaching. The sad thing is people are not living by what they perform. If you pay attention to the signs, you will see that God is coming back quicker than you think. Think about that. As we die God will pull up everything that we have done. From there he will either say "well done thy good and faithful servant" or" department from me you workers of iniquity, for I never knew you". That is deep. We never think about it. It's sad that most people will never fear God.

Repent ye therefore, and be converted, that your sins may be blotted out, when the times of refreshing shall come from the presence of the Lord.

Acts 3:19

<u>Day Fifty-Eight Reflection</u>

See That You Are A True Inspiration

Daily Prayer: Ask God to purge your heart of all your sins.

If God had come back today, would you make it to heaven (explain)?

_____
_____
_____
_____
_____
_____

What things have been deposited into your account?

_____
_____
_____
_____
_____
_____

Would you consider yourself walking with Christ?

_____
_____
_____
_____
_____
_____

Day Fifty-Nine

Thought of the day: Find that place of peace

Peace: presence and experience of right things

Do you ever wonder why there is always trouble in things that you do? There is always something on our jobs, in our homes, families, relationship, etc. There is always trouble there, because there is no peace in those areas.

According to the Old Testament, peace was completeness, soundness, and well-being of many things. Peace that Jesus spoke was a combination of hope, trust, quiet mind and soul. It is one thing to always be stressed, depressed, miserable, or worried.

For that reason you need be at peace with the way things are going. God promises us that he will give us peace. Sometimes we live our life not being able to find peace. However, God reminds us that he is the way, the truth, and the light.

God will give us rest. As the bible tells us, there was a storm out on the ocean. While Jesus was asleep the other men became afraid. Jesus only said three words. Peace be still. From there, the storms had calmed. Before he had said these words, peace was already still. He just had to proclaim it out of his mouth.

Through the storms of life, there is peace. When the king walks in there is peace. That is just the power that a king has. Too many of God's people live a miserable life or place themselves in a miserable situation. Eventually, there has to be some type of peace that will come. There are people who are in your life that you need to make peace with. Honestly, you should have peace with your past; however, due to it possibly destroying you, there has been no peace there. It has been more grief than anything. We can argue with our loved ones; however some type of peace has to come. Knowing that we have peace of things will help us get an understanding to be able to rest well in the late hours of night. It's good to have peace and to be at peace. We can watch others be confined into sickness for the rest of our life and not have peace until God has called them home. For most of us, it is some type of relief. Too many people live a miserable life that has been caused by themselves. A person can never find peace with certain things if they are not able to find it for themselves. Some people would use the excuse that they may not be happy. In fact that may be very true. It could be things like school, relationships, church, careers, or elsewhere that causes unhappiness.

   Everything will start off good, but we still need peace throughout the good. A place of peace is a place where we can have a worry free life. It's a place that is quiet to help soothe us. It can also be a place that will help the heart feel better. Some people have a peaceful place where they go to relax or get time back. When you become unhappy in life, then something needs to change. We work so much and do so many things that we will forget to allow ourselves space to have a peace of mind. Birds fly free but never have to worry. The thing I love about peace is once it has come, it will help us to feel as if we are free from many things. Concentrate on good emotions and repeating positive thoughts. People should do more things that they love to do. It will gives us a better peace of mind. As we then feel loved, it will bring us peace. Never struggle to find a place of peace. More peace causes more happiness in life. Stop stressing while God is in the process of bringing a blessing.

Peace I leave with you, my peace I give unto you: not as the world giveth, give I unto you. Let not your heart be troubled, neither let it be afraid.

John 14:27

Day Fifty-Nine Reflections

Daily Prayer: Ask God to give you peace in many things, so that you have peace in your life; whereas there will be peace with your past and people in your past.

What are some things that you must make peace with?

See That You Are A True Inspiration

Who are some people that you need to make peace with?

Why is it important for us to have peace?

What brings you peace?

True Inspiration

How will you find peace?

_____
_____
_____
_____
_____

Day Sixty

Thought of the day: Change

Change: Something given or happens over a period of time

Change is something that happens for a purpose. At some point in your life you will go through change. Most young men get super excited when they grow their first chin hair. That means the body is changing or that the young man is going through a change.

Sometimes you put things into your body, which causes your bodies to go through change. Change is good for us. As something changes, it becomes better and stronger, although sometimes you look for change in the wrong areas.

Often times we expect people to change or try to push them into changing. A person will change whenever he or she wants to. You can never press people into changing. This is a huge mistake that people make.

The key part is to understand that you can only change yourself. It shall happen for the best. During your process of changing, you are certainly growing into better people.

Everyone has to endure change. Things like losing a loved one, going through a divorce, bills, church, mistakes, or life has the ability to change a person's way of thinking and their heart. As previously stated, after going through hardships, it is always best to allow your heart time to recover and time to change.

After one has then changed, he / she will not want to go back to anything that caused grief, instead

True Inspiration *See That You Are A*

he or she will look for something better. Some of us have been stuck on the old for quite some time. I love the fact that people will make a New Year's Resolution, but sometimes they we never follow up on that list.

We always know the ones who have changed either by their attitude or personality. A person starts thinking different and doing many different things once he/she has changed. It is almost as if he or she will be creating new opportunities. The things that people fail to understand is that they must always be themselves, never allow anyone to get the best of you, change will come when we are ready, and always be yourself. Never be fake for anyone. Despite, where others like it or not, it doesn't matter. Allow change to make you feel good on the inside, but switch some things up. Be the person that God created.

Create in me a clean heart, O God; and renew a right spirit within me. Cast me not away from thy presence; and take not thy holy spirit from me.

See That You Are A True Inspiration

Restore unto me the joy of thy salvation; and uphold me with thy free spirit.

Psalms 51: 10-12

Day Sixty Reflections

Daily Prayer: Ask God to change of your heart of the things that you need to change from.

In your words, explain change

_____
_____
_____
_____
_____
_____

What could be things you need to change or work on?

_____
_____
_____
_____
_____
_____

See That You Are A True Inspiration

How would See that you are a true inspiration help you change?

_____
_____
_____
_____
_____

Explain how God helped you during this sixty day challenge?

_____
_____
_____

What were some key points that you learned?

_____
_____
_____
_____
_____

How will you begin to inspire yourself?

_____
_____
_____

True Inspiration   *See That You Are A*

_____
_____

What things inspire you in your daily endeavors?

_____
_____
_____
_____
_____

How will you be an inspiration to others?

_____
_____
_____
_____
_____

After reading this, are you able to see yourself for who you are (explain)?

_____
_____
_____

On a scale from one to ten, please explain your relationship with God and how you plan on getting closer to him?

_____

See That You Are A True Inspiration

Sources

Youngblood, Ronald; Bruce, F.F; Harrison, R.K. *Nelson's Student Bible Dictionary*. Nashville, TN: Thomas Nelson, Inc., 2005. Print

Merriam Webster's Dictionary. Springfield, Ma: Merriam-Webster's Inc., 2005. Print

King James Bible. Nashville, TN: Holman Bible Publishers, 1979. Print

Dr. Ogilvie, John Lloyd. *The complete family bible reference / concordance*. Nashville, TN: Thomas Nelson, Inc., 1982. Print

Anderson, Ken. *Where to find it in the bible (the ultimate A-Z resource)*. Nashville, TN: Thomas Nelson, Inc., 1996. Print

Greatness (empowered relationships), written by Bishop T.D Jakes. T. D Jakes Ministries. Dallas, TX. DVD

Harvey, Steve. *Act like a Success, Think like a success*. Augusta, KS: Amistad Publishing, 2014. Print

Made in the USA
Columbia, SC
09 December 2020